BRADNER LIBRARY
SCHOOLCRAFT COLLEGE
LIVONIA, MI 48152

KL 4345 .S43 1994

Sealey, Raphael.

The justice of the Greeks

The Justice of the Greeks

The Justice of the Greeks

Raphael Sealey

Ann Arbor
The University of Michigan Press

Copyright © by the University of Michigan 1994
All rights reserved
Published in the United States of America by
The University of Michigan Press
Manufactured in the United States of America
∞ Printed on acid-free paper

1997 1996 1995 1994   4 3 2 1

A CIP catalogue record for this book is available from the British Library.

Library of Congress Cataloging-in-Publication Data

Sealey, Raphael.
    The justice of the Greeks / Raphael Sealey.
      p.   cm.
    Includes bibliographical references and index.
    ISBN 0-472-10524-8 (alk. paper)
    1. Justice, Administration of (Greek law) 2. Rule of law (Greek law) 3. Law, Greek—Interpretation and construction. 4. Law, Greek—Language.   I. Title.
KL4345.S43 1994
340.5′38—dc20   94-8111
                                                                                 CIP

*To
Dorte-Freyja Sealey*

Allez daz ir habt vernomen,
daz ist gar ein wint: nū frāget mich.
   —Walther von der Vogelweide

Preface

This book is an inquiry into the rule of law. It inquires in particular into Greek thought in relation to the rule of law. It maintains that law or justice, as envisaged when people recognize the rule of law, springs from normative ideas embedded in the Indo-European vocabulary and that those ideas were first given practical and institutional effect by the Greeks of antiquity. It admits that further steps in the direction to which Greeks had pointed were taken by Romans and have been taken by others since. But those steps are the subject for other books.

This book also arises from reflection on questions of method. It is written in the conviction that philology is necessary but not enough. A study of words in their contexts may lead far, but more distance remains to be covered. The additional method, pursued here alongside philology, may be called the comparative and theoretical study of law, for want of a more precise word. The meaning of the term may become clear in the chapters.

Caution must be observed, if one entertains reflections on method. Generally, if a historian wishes to devote a book to method, he would be well advised not to do so. If he thinks that he knows something about method, he would be wise to write about problems and apply his knowledge to them. The test of a method is its success in solving problems. If on the other hand he engages in an overt discussion of method, he cannot avoid saying what he finds deficient in the methods of his predecessors. So without throwing light on problems, he will merely show what a cantankerous curmudgeon he is.

The method pursued here has been learned, well or badly, from predecessors, especially from the late H.J. Wolff and from E. Ruschenbusch and G. Thür. I believe that the work of these scholars deserves wider recognition in North America than it has received. Naturally they are not to blame for present shortcomings.

It has been a pleasure to expound some of the ideas in two lectures. One was delivered in the University of Konstanz in June 1989. The other was the Loeb lecture at Harvard University in April 1991. I thank my hosts, Professors W. Schuller, R.J. Tarrant, and E. Badian, and the audiences for patient hearing and comments.

It is also a pleasure to thank Dr. Ellen Bauerle of the University of Michigan Press. She received a manuscript that still needed significant improvement and led me patiently forward.

Contents

Abbreviations		xiii
Chapter 1.	Scope of the Inquiry	1
Chapter 2.	Codes and Compilations of Law	25
Chapter 3.	The Unity of Greek Law	59
Chapter 4.	How to Resolve Disputes I: Greece	91
Chapter 5.	How to Resolve Disputes II: Athens	113
Chapter 6.	To Each His Due	133
Bibliography		157
Index		161

Abbreviations

The abbreviations employed for ancient authors and their works are easy to recognize. Fragments of Solon's laws are cited from Ruschenbusch, *Solonos Nomoi*.

ABSA	*Annual of the British School at Athens*
AJAH	*American Journal of Ancient History*
AJP	*American Journal of Philology*
CJ	*Classical Journal*
CQ	*Classical Quarterly*
CR	*Classical Review*
EMC	*Echos du Monde Classique = Classical Views*
F Gr Hist	*Fragmente der griechischen Historiker*
GRBS	*Greek, Roman, and Byzantine Studies*
IC	*Inscriptiones Creticae*
IG	*Inscriptiones Graecae*
JHS	*Journal of Hellenic Studies*
RE	*Real-Enzyclopädie der klassischen Altertumswissenschaft*
RFIC	*Rivista di Filologia e di Istruzione Classica*
RIDA	*Revue Internationale des Droits de l'Antiquité*
SEG	*Supplementum Epigraphicum Graecum*
SIG	*Sylloge Inscriptionum Graecarum³*
TAPhA	*Transactions of the American Philological Association*
ZPE	*Zeitschrift für Papyrologie und Epigraphik*
ZSR	*Zeitschrift der Savigny-Stiftung für Rechtsgeschichte, Romanistische Abteilung*

CHAPTER 1

Scope of the Inquiry

"Law," "justice," "right," and related concepts have a peculiar status in current speech. They are both familiar and strange to the practical man, as he goes about his everyday business. Let it be supposed, for example, that he goes to a store and buys a radio receiver. He looks at various receivers offered for sale and chooses one of them. He hands money to the dealer and the latter in return hands him the receiver and a written receipt. The purchaser takes the receiver home, plugs it into an electric outlet, and listens to the news twice each day. So far it might not occur to him to recognize that the law has played any part in his activity.

The story may, however, have a less happy ending. Suppose that after two days the radio receiver ceases to function. It becomes stubbornly silent. Thereupon the purchaser takes it back to the dealer. The latter asks the customer to wait a few minutes and takes the radio receiver to the workbench in another part of his store. Ten minutes later he comes back with sprightly step, returns the apparatus to the purchaser and assures him that it will work well henceforth. Perhaps he explains that a little wire had not been properly affixed. The purchaser takes the receiver home, and if he remains contented, he may still have no occasion to think about law.

Yet the story may have a less satisfactory outcome, if the radio receiver breaks down repeatedly, or if the dealer refuses to repair it. Possibly the two men will engage in an altercation and come to blows. Then a bystander may call the police and thus the criminal law intervenes. Yet even if there is no breach of the peace, the disagreement may become so acute that one of the parties sues the other in a civil court. If the object in dispute, such as a radio receiver, is only of modest value, the dispute could be taken in many modern cities to a "court for small claims," as it is called, and receive summary settlement. But in principle, or if the object has great value, the dispute can go to a regular court and many questions can arise—for example: is the seller only liable for defects that appear promptly after the sale, or is he still liable even if a defect first appears six months later? In the latter case, can he be required to refund the original price or only the value that the object retains after six months?[1] Again, it can happen that a dissatisfied purchaser addresses himself to the police, and if there are serious grounds of suspicion, criminal proceedings for fraud are opened against the dealer or manufacturer.

As the possible stories about sale of a radio receiver indicate, the purchaser is only likely to think about law when he meets with misfortune. Yet the law can only help him, because it supplied the framework within which the original transaction took place. That is, the law can only make itself felt in eventual disputes because it was tacitly present at the original moment of purchase and sale, when there was not yet any expectation of a dispute. In modern custom the tacit presence of the law at that time is often made manifest in the written receipt, which the seller hands to the purchaser.

The practical man is likely to recognize the presence of the law in the rare and important occurrences of his life, even if no dispute arises. If he buys a house, he or his agent may carry out a formal conveyance. If he makes a will, he will probably seek expert guidance and hence make sure that the required number of witnesses are present and any other needed forms are observed. If he marries a wife, he will probably recognize that he is observing the positive law in ascertaining that he is free to marry, in securing a specific number of witnesses, and in carrying out registration. When a child is born, the parents usually know that registration of the birth is a legal act. Much the same can be said about attainment of majority. In some countries it used to be customary for parents to give their child a key to the door of the house when the child attained the age of twenty-one years. At least some of those countries have since altered the age of majority to eighteen. Therefore parents are

---

1. Starting from the edict of the curule aediles, Roman jurists developed the law of seller's liability; see R.W. Leage, *Roman Private Law,* 3d ed., rev. A.M. Prichard (London: Macmillan, 1961), 360-61; and see B. Nicholas, *An Introduction to Roman Law* (Oxford: Oxford University Press, 1962), 181-82.

probably even more aware that the age is determined by the law of their community and it could be different.

In short, the practical man recognizes the presence of the law when he enters into a dispute and when he performs major transactions, but the law encompasses him on many other occasions in addition to those. A moment's reflection on lines indicated in the preceding paragraphs may convince him that the law plays a part whenever he deals with another person. Yet even this concept of the scope of law may be too narrow. Perhaps the law is present even when a man does something which has a bearing only on himself. Some systems of law forbid suicide, and it is not certain that such systems have strayed beyond their field of competence. Gaius the jurist mentions measures of the emperor Antoninus Pius to restrict the severity exercised by a master over his own slaves, and Gaius expresses approval "because we ought not to make bad use of our own right" (1.53). Law appears to be present everywhere. Yet the provisions of the law are not the same in all communities. The age of majority, the degree of freedom of bequest, the conditions to be fulfilled in contracting marriage, and the seller's liability for defects in his wares vary from one system of positive law to another. One may well begin to wonder what this mysterious thing, law (or justice, or right), is; what is meant by saying that such and such a practice is "the law"?

Bewilderment increases if one scrutinizes *law* and related words in English and languages that, through cultural propinquity, have contributed to English concepts. The English word *law* has two senses, well distinguished in the *Oxford English Dictionary:*

1. *a.* The body of rules, whether proceeding from formal enactment or from custom, which a particular state or community recognizes as binding on its members or subjects. (In this sense usually *the law.*)
2. *a.* One of the individual rules which constitute the "law" (sense 1) of a state or polity. In early use only *pl.* The plural has often a collective sense (after L. jura, leges) approaching sense 1.

Although one may wonder what semantic history lies concealed in preferences for the plural, the distinction is easy to grasp. Law in sense 1 is a body of law, such as the law of property or Roman law. Sense 2 comes into play when a legislature votes for a bill and thereby makes it a law (or act).

Sense 1 is represented in Latin by *ius,* in French by *droit,* and in German by *Recht.* Sense 2, a law as an individual rule, appears in Latin as *lex* (and in other guises), in French as *loi,* and in German as *Gesetz.* But the words bearing sense 1 are not easy to pin down. The German example will suffice as an illustration. *Recht* can indeed be a body of law.[2] But, second, it can be a right in such expressions as "The householder has a right to plant onions in his front garden,"[3] and, third, it can be justice in such expressions as "justice was on his side."[4] In the second meaning of *Recht* English cannot substitute "(the) law" for "right"; it is not intelligible to say: "The householder has a law (or: the law) to plant onions in his front garden." Evidently "law" (as a body of law) and *Recht* overlap but do not coincide. Furthermore, in the third meaning, English can substitute "right" or "the law" for "justice"; one can say "right was on his side" or "the law was on his side" and be understood without difficulty. Thus the English words "law," "right," and "justice" embrace a range of meanings covered also by *Gesetz* and *Recht* (or by *loi* and *droit*). But the distribution of the meanings between the words differs from one language to another. There is a common semantic field, but its components differ and one may wonder whether its boundaries are the same in the different languages.

If, however, the practical man, whose native language happens to be English, settles in Germany, he needs to learn the language. But once he has a modest fluency, he can perform many legal transactions—such as buying a radio receiver or a house, marrying, registering the birth of a child, and even making a will—without seeking instruction from a German professor of law. He may be unable to give a reasoned account of the concept of law or of justice or of right in any language, yet mere linguistic competence enables him to operate with that concept successfully.

Philosophic inquiries have tried to clarify the nature of law (or justice

---

2. "Gesamtheit der staatlich festgelegten bzw. anerkannten Normen des menschlichen, insbes. gesellschaftlichen Verhaltens; Gesamtheit der Gesetze u. gesetzähnlichen Normen; Rechtsordnung" (Duden, *Das grosse Wörterbuch der deutschen Sprache,* 1980).

3. "Berechtigter, von Rechts wegen zuerkannter Anspruch; Berechtigung oder Befugnis" (ibid.). In this sense the term *subjektives Recht* is employed by jurists; see P. Bähr, *Grundzüge des bürgerlichen Rechts,* 7th ed. (Munich: Vahlen, 1989), 37.

4. "Das, was recht, dem Recht [sempfinden] gemäss ist; Berechtigung, wie sie das Recht [sempfinden] zuerkannt." Duden, *Das grosse Wörterbuch;* examples offered in Duden include "Das Recht war auf seiner Seite."

or right). An old theory said that there existed something called the law of nature. It was supposedly common to all men, and they could ascertain it because they had reason. If any positive law of a given community conflicted with natural law, that positive law was not valid. It followed that the body of law current in a community derived its validity from natural law. Cicero endorsed this theory and said that he had learned it from Greek philosophers. Where he said that natural law was common to all mankind, Roman jurists later made it common to men and animals; they offered the union of male and female as an example of its provisions.[5]

The theory of natural law continued to be widely held into the eighteenth century. It is attractive because it offers a seemingly satisfactory account of situations where people say that a type of conduct is allowed, or even prescribed by the positive law, but not just. If, for example, a rich farmer died, leaving three adult sons, traditional English law assigned the whole inheritance to the eldest son and left nothing to the other two. It is easy to say that this rule of primogeniture is unjust. It is more difficult to say what is meant by calling the rule unjust. The criticism is not a mere expression of sentiment; "primogeniture is unjust" does not mean "I dislike primogeniture." Again, to say that primogeniture is legal but inequitable or immoral offers a mere word, where something more is required. The theory of natural law purports to offer something more than a word, and in criticizing primogeniture (and some other institutions) the theorist can observe that the rule he advocates, such as equal division of the inheritance among the sons, is observed in many communities; so it becomes plausible to say that the preferred rule is common to all mankind. On the other hand the theory of natural law is unsatisfactory because one cannot discover what nature is or how its precepts are to be ascertained.[6] Moreover, it fails to explain why

---

5. Cic. *de legg.* 1.17-39, 56; 2.8-13; Just. *Inst.* 1.2 pr.
6. Cf. C. Milosz: *The Captive Mind* (New York: Knopf, 1953), 25-26: ("Man tends to regard the order he lives in as *natural*. The houses he passes on his way to work seem more like rocks rising out of the earth than like products of human hands." The whole passage on pp. 25-29 is apposite here.) Drawing on the related ideas of natural law and social contract, Rawls has propounded a theory that has rightly won a great deal of respect. It rests, however, on a notion of rational choice: "The intuitive idea of justice as fairness is to think of the first principles of justice as themselves the object of an original agreement in a suitably defined initial situation. These principles are those which rational persons concerned to advance their interests would accept in this position of equality to settle the basic terms of their association. J. Rawls, *A Theory of Justice* (Cambridge, MA: Belknap, 1971), 118. The rational has not been defined. What, for example, is the rational choice for the parent of a child to make, if an advantage can be enjoyed by one of them but

different communities have different systems of law. Diversity of law demands a historical explanation.

Although the theory of natural law was propounded by the Greek philosophers on whom Cicero drew, it is not a serviceable instrument for understanding Greek law, since it lacks a historical dimension. Two other theories have been developed more recently and they are more promising. The one was the work of John Austin (1790–1859), who acknowledged his debt to Hobbes and Bentham. After his death his theory had extensive influence in England and the United States. The other theory was offered by Friedrich Carl von Savigny (1779–1861); he was professor at Berlin from the foundation of the university in 1809.

Austin's theory is sometimes summarized in the maxim that law is the command of a sovereign. With greater care he himself wrote:

> Every positive law (or every law simply and strictly so called) is set, directly or circuitously, by a sovereign individual or body, to a member or members of the independent political society wherein its author is supreme.

This account invites the question, What is a sovereign? Austin gave his answer:

> Defining sovereignty and independent political society (or stating their characters or distinguishing marks), I have said that a given society is a society political and independent, if the bulk or generality of its members habitually obey the commands of a determinate and independent party.[7]

These two utterances incur a risk of circularity: a law is to be obeyed because it is the order of a sovereign and a sovereign is a person or body that is obeyed. Even so, Austin's theory has the merit of recognizing the coercive element in law. A sympathetic critic has summarized the theory by saying that in Austin's view, law is "an order backed by threats."[8]

---

not by both? In other words, does rationality demand solicitude for the person or for the species?

7. J. Austin, *The Province of Jurisprudence Determined*. The quotations are from pp. 350 and 356 of the edition published by The Noonday Press (New York: 1954). The first edition appeared in 1832.

8. H.L.A. Hart, *The Concept of Law* (Oxford: Oxford University Press, 1961), 6. Hart

The theory gives a tolerable account of criminal statutes, that is, of those laws that have been deliberately enacted to define and penalize offenses, although it does not explain why the laws of crime can be imposed even on the legislators who enacted them. But criminal law is only a small part of law. The law of inheritance, the body of law that tells people whether they can marry and how they can set about doing so, the law authorizing people to enter into contracts and stating conditions under which a contract may cease to be valid, these and many other branches of law cannot be reduced to orders backed by threats. For example, part of the law of inheritance authorizes a man to make a will; it tells him the conditions that must be fulfilled and how to make a will. It does not order him to make a will or penalize him for not making one. If he does not conform to the requirements, his will may be invalid, but invalidity is not a penalty inflicted on the testator after death; it is a misfortune suffered by his designated heirs.

These and other defects in Austin's theory are now widely recognized. Yet the theory calls for note in the present inquiry because it has an affinity with some studies of Greek law. Austin's theory reduces law to a part of the positive law of a given community at a given time. It is in harmony with the practice of those historians who are content to ascertain, as far as possible, the rules valid in each Greek city and who assume that any changes occurring were made by deliberate enactment. Austin's theory is ahistorical in that it does not admit that law may change by any means other than statutory enactment. It does not recognize that law may be in a constant state of flux.

Savigny recognized the historical element in law. He expounded his programmatic ideas in a short treatise, *On the calling of our age for legislation and for the science of law*,[9] first published in 1814. He opposed

---

summarizes criticisms of Austin on p. 77. It need scarcely be said that I am much indebted to Hart's book for my understanding of Austin. Theorists within the Anglo-American tradition have been preoccupied with the coercive element in law, for example: "Our discussions about law by and large assume, I suggest, that the most abstract and fundamental point of legal practice is to guide and constrain the power of government in the following way. Law insists that force not be used or withheld, no matter how useful that would be to ends in view, except as licensed or required by individual rights and responsibilities flowing from past political decisions about when collective force is justified." R. Dworkin, *Law's Empire* (Cambridge, MA: Belknap, 1986), 93. Chapter 4 will pay attention to the part played in the growth of law by ways of settling disputes where there is no governmental coercion.

9. Savigny, *Vom Beruf unsrer Zeit für Gesetzgebung und Rechtswissenschaft*, 3d ed., enl. (Heidelberg, 1840). An assessment of Savigny's significance is offered by H. Kantor-

the theory of natural law, of which the leading protagonist was A.F.J. Thibaut at Heidelberg. Savigny recognized that in the middle of the eighteenth century people had looked for a universally valid system of law, to be applied mechanically, but now happily that quest had been abandoned, since people had acquired a historical sense. Savigny rejected also the view of those jurists who supposed that the body of law (*Recht*) springs wholly from the particular laws (*Gesetze*) current in the community; on that view (which coincides with the theory propounded later by Austin) the body of law could be altered in haste and the task of the jurist was merely to expound the particular laws. Savigny objected that that view paid no heed to "customary law" (*Gewohnheitsrecht*), and he noted that it was often combined with a belief in natural law.

In positive terms Savigny maintained that civil law, like language and the constitution, springs from the distinctive character of the nation. So like language, law is constantly changing, but it remains true to "the nature and the character of the nation" (*das Wesen und der Charakter des Volkes*). At an early stage the fundamentals of the law are expressed through formal actions, such as those the early Roman jurists applied; later, as at the present, the fundamentals are explicit principles, which are articulated in speech and writing. "It has been asserted above that the proper seat of the law is the common consciousness of the nation."[10] But when law becomes elaborated, it becomes difficult to trace the consciousness of the nation, and so the law is entrusted to "the consciousness of the jurists," who represent the nation. The law continues to develop at two levels, which interact. The one level is the consciousness of the nation, where the political element operates, and the other is the science cultivated by jurists, among whom the technical element comes into play. For the law continues to develop not from the arbitrary intervention of a legislator but from its own internal causes. The practical conclusion that Savigny drew was that codification was not the right way to achieve security in the law and community in Germany in his time; "I recognize the right means in a science of law which progresses organically and can be common to the whole nation."[11]

---

owicz, "Savigny and the Historical School of Law," *Law Quarterly Review* 53 (1937): 326–43.

10. Savigny, *Vom Beruf,* 11: "Es ist nämlich oben behauptet worden, dass der eigentliche Sitz des Rechts das gemeinsame Bewusstseyn des Volkes sey." My summary in this paragraph is based on Savigny's second chapter (8–15).

11. Ibid., 161: "Ich sehe das rechte Mittel in einer organisch fortschreitenden Rechtswissenschaft, die der ganzen Nation gemein seyn kann."

A facile criticism of Savigny's view complains that the nature and character of a nation cannot be defined, located, or recognized with any confidence; even the word *nation* is ambivalent, since it refers sometimes to political power and sometimes to cultural tradition. But this criticism can be rebutted. A nation can be understood as a *Schicksalsgemeinschaft* or community of people experiencing common historical fortunes (there is no single English word for this concept). This definition is not wholly precise, but many words serviceable in the study of history include an area of imprecision; they may even be serviceable for that very reason. The words *nature* and *character* (of the nation) may perhaps be discarded as somewhat romantic, and instead one may say that in Savigny's view law springs from the historical circumstances of the nation. Thus reformulated, Savigny's theory insists that a system of law is tied to its nation and that law develops, not from the detached and in principle arbitrary choices of a legislative organ, but from the historical experience of the nation.

Savigny's theory has, however, been criticized on more precise grounds, and three of them call for note.[12] First, statutory enactment by a legislative organ acting in some degree of detachment from the rest of the community can change or even create law. This fact is too well known to need illustration or brook denial. Yet it is accompanied by another fact, not so widely recognized but easy to establish. Statutory legislation often has effects that were not foreseen and that differ markedly from the purposes that the legislation was designed to accomplish. For example, in Victorian England the act of parliament penalizing homosexual behavior proved to be the blackmailer's charter. Again, the Eighteenth Amendment to the Constitution of the United States had the effect of creating a great opportunity for organized crime, although it only talked about prohibiting the manufacture, sale, and transportation of intoxicating liquors. Examples could be multiplied. The good intentions of legislators have often had disastrous consequences. Surely the disasters have occurred because the new statute came into conflict with the legal tradition of the community. Savigny's theory can account for this phenomenon of conflict and disaster, because he insisted that the proper means to reform was "a science of law which progresses organically." New law, then, should spring from the consciousness of the nation or from the consciousness of jurists who represent the nation.

---

12. These criticisms are drawn in substance from Kantorowicz, "Savigny and the Historical School of Law," but the formulation is mine.

A second criticism arises from legal transplant. Sometimes one community has adopted a whole system of law from another community. The Code of Napoleon has become current in many places outside France. The German Code, which came into force in 1900 (often called the Code of 1896, from the year when the work of drawing it up was completed) has also been adopted elsewhere and even in Japan. Systems embodied in a code are relatively easy to borrow; the borrowing nation has only to buy a book, albeit a large book, and make some modifications. The English Common Law, on the other hand, is not embodied in a code but in legal memory that preserves precedents.[13] To adopt it, the borrowing nation has the more difficult task of transplanting lawyers. Yet even that has been accomplished, for example, in Cyprus (through no fault of the Cypriots).

Study of legal transplant in mediaeval France has thrown light on the phenomenon. Sometimes the people of a city found that their rules were uncertain. So they adopted a body of rules from another city, esteemed for its good laws, or from Roman or canon law. Sometimes the citizens of the borrowing city believed that the rules adopted were their own ancestral customs.[14] The process was much like that of the extensive adoption of the *Sachsenspiegel* in the thirteenth century. Eike von Repchow, a private person experienced in the practice of the courts, compiled a "book

---

13. In modern American usage the expression "[systems of] the Common Law" means English law and systems derived from it, including those of the United States (with a partial exception in Louisiana) and those of countries of the Commonwealth; these have accepted relatively little influence from Roman law and they rely consciously and extensively on precedent as a source of law. The expression "[systems of] the Civil Law" means systems current in many countries on the continent of Europe, including France, Germany, Italy, and Spain. These have been influenced in varying degrees by Roman law and they rely predominantly on a code as the source of law. Yet this statement of the contrast exaggerates it. German lawyers draw on "the interpretive practice of the courts" as a source of law; it has been fruitful in developing the branch of law called "the general law of personality"; see Bähr, *Grundzüge des bürgerlichen Rechts,* 9 and 39.

The Hellenist who wishes to draw on another system as a basis of comparison for Greek institutions will probably find it easier to grasp ideas drawn from Roman and Civil Law than those characteristic of the Common Law. One can, for example, make comparisons successfully in the belief that a person may own a parcel of land. But in English law one does not own land; one owns at most "the estate in fee simple absolute in possession" (Henrich, *Einführung in das englische Privatrecht,* 2d ed. [Darmstadt: Wissenschaftliche Buchgesellschaft, 1993], 90). On closer scrutiny, but only on closer scrutiny, the Roman and Civil concept of owning things may prove to be problematic (Nicholas, *Introduction to Roman Law,* 153-57).

14. A. Watson, *The Evolution of Law* (Baltimore: Johns Hopkins University Press, 1985), 53-54, cf. 59.

of law" (*Rechtsbuch*), first in Latin and later with enlargements in Low German, the latter version being called the *Sachsenspiegel*. He drew on local practices and tried to harmonize and modify them in order to produce a practical handbook.[15] Courts and administrators adopted his book; they were glad to have something to draw on in their uncertainties.

The Japanese adoption of the German Code would appear to be in principle similar. A desire had arisen for a modern system of law, and so a foreign system with a clear statement was transplanted. Except in cases of foreign conquest, legal transplant is only likely to occur if the borrowing nation has discovered that its current practices are unsatisfactory. Similar causes brought about the reception of Roman law in mediaeval Europe.[16] It must be admitted that the phenomenon of legal transplant is a serious obstacle to the theory of Savigny. Even with modifications, the German Code did not spring from the nature and character of the Japanese nation. At best the theory can only accommodate transplant by subsuming it under the historical circumstances of the nation, but to do so diminishes the content of the theory.

A third criticism addresses the notion of "customary law," which plays a not insignificant part in Savigny's ideas. People often say that law springs from custom, and this assertion is easy to accept, but on scrutiny custom proves to be elusive. Mere repetition of a practice has no normative force. Many travelers may bring dutiable goods surreptitiously past customs officers without paying duty, but smuggling does not in consequence become lawful. The jurists employed by Justinian recognized unwritten custom as a source of law. The recognition was much to their credit, since their system relied predominantly on written law. Being aware that the normative force of custom required explanation, they sought an explanation in the consent of the people who observed the custom.[17] But this account stretches the meaning of consent. A theory that is easier to defend says that custom becomes law when it is upheld by the decision of a court.[18] But if so, surely one could say more succinctly that law is the decisions of the courts and custom has no role to play.

Let it be admitted that the criticisms have some force. Savigny's theory has defects; it does not succeed as a complete account of the nature of

---

15. K. von Amira and K.A. Eckhardt, *Germanisches Recht* (Berlin: de Gruyter, 1960), 1:154-68.
16. This process is now far less mysterious, thanks to Watson, *Evolution*, 66-97.
17. Just. *Inst.* 1.2.9.
18. Watson, *Evolution*, 43-65, especially 49-50, 54-59.

law. Even so it has the merit of recognizing that law can develop without statutory enactment and that the development stays within limits or follows lines that can be discerned. To illustrate the bearing of these insights on matters of ancient law three institutions, Greek and in part Roman, will now be reviewed. They are *atimia*, universal succession, and the *epiklēros*. They have been selected because, however strange to modern systems of the Common Law, they are embedded thoroughly in their native systems.

Atimia

Addressing the assembled Athenians in 342/1 B.C., Demosthenes exhorted them to follow the example of their ancestors. Long ago, when Arthmios of Zeleia had brought Persian bribes to Greece, the Athenians had declared him and his descendants enemies and *atimoi*. The orator had to add some words of explanation:

> This does not mean the *atimia* of which one would speak ordinarily. For what difference did it make to a man of Zeleia, if he was not to take part in the common things of the Athenians? But in the laws on homicide, in reference to acts for which no judicial hearing is granted but one may kill the culprit without incurring guilt, it is written: "And let him be killed *atimos*." This means that anyone who kills one of those culprits is pure. (9.44)

There is no need to ask here whether the decree allegedly passed against Arthmios long before was genuine. Nor need one pause over the oddity that, except in this passage, *atimia* is attested in Athens only as a penalty imposed on citizens. What calls for note is that *atimia* had changed, as Demosthenes explained, and in his explanation he did not cite any statutory enactment.

Atimia, which will require attention in chapter 5, deprived an Athenian of the protection of the courts. Consequently his enemies could harm him to any degree with impunity. At first public authority took note only of misdeeds that were few and large. So a culprit deprived of protection was likely to have enemies who would harm him, unless he made good his escape into the safety of exile. Later public authority advanced into more spheres of activity and it imposed *atimia* for many offenses. Some of these did not arouse indignation either among personal enemies or in the general public. In particular a citizen who owed a financial debt to the state and did not pay it by the ninth prytany of the year became *atimos*. By the time of Demosthenes many of the *atimoi* were public debtors. If such a man refrained from making enemies or drawing attention to himself, he might in fact remain in Athens, even though he had been deprived of the protection of the courts. The audience of Demosthenes was accustomed to *atimia* in its milder effect. So he had to explain that it had changed in character. In doing so he drew attention to its occurrence in its pristine character in the laws on homicide, which continued in force.[19]

Other societies have institutionalized means whereby the law can be developed without recourse to statute. In Rome this task was the province of juriconsults. They gave opinions on questions of law. The degree of their authority was not clear, but only a bold man would challenge the opinion of a juriconsult, unless he had another juriconsult of at least equal prestige to back him up with a contrary opinion. The science practised by the juriconsults came to be articulated, developed, and respected in the course of the first century B.C.[20] Modern societies often concede the task of developing the law to an organized profession of lawyers. The Athenians did not have legal experts. But they could engage, perhaps on a more modest scale, in characteristically legal ways of thinking. That such a mode of thought could operate in the development of the law in Athens is illustrated by the remark of Demosthenes on *atimia*.

Universal Succession

The Roman law of inheritance starts from the concept of a *universitas iuris*, as it is sometimes called. At any time in his adult life, including the moment of his death, a man has a bundle of rights and obligations. They may be very disparate. They are held together by the sole fact that they are the totality of the rights and obligations of one person. Starting from this concept, Roman law tries to replace the dead man with an heir or heirs, who will assume his whole legal personality as it was at

---

19. Ruschenbusch recognized that the change was not made by statute but came about by practice; see E. Ruschenbusch, *Untersuchungen zur Geschichte des athenischen Strafrechts* (Cologne: Böhlau, 1968), 11–12, 16–29; cf. R. Sealey, "How Citizenship and the City Began in Athens," *AJAH* 8 (1983): 98–101, 105–11.

20. Much light has been thrown on this by Frier, *Rise of the Roman Jurists: Studies in Cicero's "pro Caecina"* (Princeton: Princeton University Press, 1985).

the time of his death. This goal could be achieved by a will or by rules of intestate succession; the primary function of a Roman will was to name an heir or heirs.[21] In addition to acquiring things from the deceased person, the Roman *heres* performed the tasks that are assigned to an executor in modern systems of the Common Law.

Testamentary bequest was at least as old in Rome as the Twelve Tables. In and after the classical period a will could take various forms and there was flexibility in content. A man might bequeath his property in specified shares, equal or unequal, to several heirs. After naming an heir or heirs, he could assign legacies to further persons. Again, the praetors and later Justinian devised ways to save an heir from an inheritance in which the liabilities exceeded the assets (a *damnosa hereditas*). Even so, the idea of a universal succession continued to dominate the law, and its dominance can be illustrated from a consequence that may be strange to people accustomed to systems of the Common Law. Suppose that a man made a will bequeathing a numerically specified part—a half, for example—of his property to a named heir but said nothing about the rest. Then in Roman law the named heir inherited the whole inheritance, since the law recognized him as heir and looked for an heir to take over the whole bundle of rights and duties. This consequence illustrated the principle: "No one can die partly testate and partly intestate." In the Common Law, on the other hand, the heir named in the will to part of the estate receives his share and the rest passes according to the rules of intestate succession.[22]

Athenian law had a concept similar to universal succession. Speeches delivered in lawsuits about inheritance employ the word *oikos* for the

---

21. Gaius 2.97-99; Just. *Inst.* 2.9.6; Leage, *Roman Private Law,* 233-34; Nicholas, *Introduction to Roman Law,* 235-37. A few rights belonged solely to one person and were extinguished by his death. If, for example, A had a usufruct in a thing belonging to B, the usufruct ceased at A's death, and B's ownership was no longer encumbered (Just. *Inst.* 2.4.3-4; Nicholas, *Introduction to Roman Law,* 145). Again, if A inflicted *iniuria* (contumelious disregard of rights of personality) on B, the essence of the offense was insult (*contumelia*) and the insult was suffered only by the one person; so B's right to recover a delictal payment from A ceased at B's death (Gaius 3.220-25; Just. *Inst.* 4.4; Leage, *Roman Private Law,* 416-19; Nicholas, *Introduction to Roman Law,* 215-16). The insistence on taking care of all the rights and obligations of the deceased by assigning them to an heir or heirs is still the starting point of the German law of inheritance; see Bähr, *Grundzüge des bürgerlichen Rechts,* 390.

22. Nicholas, *Introduction to Roman Law,* 236-37 ("Nemo pro parte testatus pro parte intestatus decedere potest"). The rule could operate if a man made a will, naming an heir to a stated proportion of his property and assigning the rest in specified legacies, but then acquired more property before dying.

whole property of the deceased. It may be encumbered, for example, with a debt to the state, with a private debt, or with an obligation to support daughters or minor sons. Usually the prose of the Attic orators reserves the word *oikos* for one man's whole bundle of rights and obligations; so it is distinct from *oikia,* which means "house." But the etymological link was palpable, and in the Greek of Homer and of the tragedians *oikos* was used for "house." Forensic speeches often mention care taken to ensure that an *oikos* should not become "empty" (*erēmos*). It would be empty if there were no man to administer the property or fulfill the obligations. One of the mandatory items on the agenda of ten of the forty meetings of the assembly each year was "the claims to inheritances (*klēroi*) and heiresses (*epiklēroi*), so that nothing may become empty without anyone's notice."[23]

Testamentary bequest in Athens was scarcely distinguishable from adoption. The same law, attributed to Solon, was used to regulate both practices.[24] It provided that, under stated conditions, a man could name an heir by will or adopt him as a son. The most restrictive of the conditions was that a man could only bequeath or adopt if he had no begotten sons. This restriction was respected in a further law, made to meet the predicament of a father who learned that his death was approaching and knew that his sons were minors; the law provided that the will should be valid if the sons did not survive to two years past puberty.[25] Yet the practice of bequest developed beyond the restriction. Several Athenian wills of the fourth and early third century are known—those of Konon, of the elder Demosthenes, of Pasion, of Plato, of Aristotle, of Epikouros[26]—and some of them exercise greater freedom. For example, the elder Demosthenes left a widow, a son aged seven, and

---

23. Ar. *AP.* 43.4. The concept has been clarified by D.M. MacDowell, "The *Oikos* in Athenian Law," *CQ,* n.s., 39 (1989): 10–21; cf. R. Sealey, *The Athenian Republic: Democracy or the Rule of Law?* (University Park: Pennsylvania State University Press, 1987), 25–26.

24. [Dem.] 46.14; cf. 44.68; Dem. 20.102; Ar. *AP.* 35.2; Plut. *Sol.* 21.3. Controversy has arisen on the question, whether the law was designed for bequest and applied to *adoptio inter vivos* (E. Ruschenbusch, "*Diatithesthai ta heautou.* Ein Beitrag zum sogenannten Testamentsgesetz des Solon," *ZSR* 79 [1962]: 307–11), or developed in the converse direction (L. Gernet, *Droit et société dans la Grèce ancienne* [Paris 1955]: 121–49).

25. [Dem.] 46.24.

26. Konon: Lys. 19.39. Demosthenes: Dem. 27.4–5. Pasion: Dem. 36.33–35; 45.27–28. Plato: Diog. L. 3.41–43. Aristotle: Diog. L. 5.11–16. Epikouros: Diog. L. 10.16–21. Also, speeches on disputes about inheritance provide brief reports of wills, for example that of Dikaiogenes (Isai. 5.5–6).

a daughter aged five. The will named three guardians who were to administer the property and care for these dependents, and it assigned legacies to encourage the guardians in conscientious performance of their trust. After the younger Demosthenes came of age, he sued his guardians by alleging embezzlement. He did not argue that the will should be disregarded because he had survived to two years beyond puberty.

The attested wills show that the legal restrictions on freedom of bequest were not fully enforced. This does not imply that additional laws had been passed to mitigate the restrictions. The proper inference is that wills that went beyond the restrictions were respected, if the interested parties were satisfied with their inheritances and legacies. In many societies freedom of bequest has developed, not because parents wished to disinherit their children, but because, like the elder Demosthenes, they wished to meet the complexity of their familial predicament in a manner more efficient than the rigid rules of intestate succession.

Less information has been preserved about the history of the law of succession in Athens than in Rome. Furthermore, the Roman conquest of Greece, followed after a long interval by the spread of Roman law, put an end to the development of native institutions. But the concept of an *oikos,* to be inherited by natural or adopted heirs, amounts to much the same thing as the universal succession of the Romans, even though the etymological image ("house") is different. It will not be amiss to note here that the Roman law of succession reveals at its most basic level an underlying concept, that of a *universitas iuris,* and a corresponding aim, that an heir or heirs should be found to take care of the assets and meet the obligations of the dead man. The same idea is revealed in the care taken by the Athenians to ensure that an *oikos* should not become empty. Concepts and corresponding aims will require further attention.

The *Epiklēros*

If a male Athenian died leaving a daughter but no sons, his property (his *oikos*) passed to his nearest male kinsman according to a fixed order, and the same heir was required to marry the orphaned daughter. The order of succession to the daughter was the same as the order of succession to the property.[27] The nearest heir had a choice; he could refuse

---

27. For the order of succession to the daughter see [Dem.] 43.51; cf. Isai. 3.72–73; 10.4–5. For the order of succession to property see Isai. 11.1–3.

the property and the woman, and then they would pass to the next heir, but an heir could not accept the one without the other. If the heir was already married, he could refuse the property and the woman or he could take them both after divorcing his wife.[28] When the heir had married the female orphan and taken the inheritance, he administered the property but he could not alienate it. It passed to the sons whom the orphan bore him when they were two years past puberty and they were required to support their mother.[29]

The orphaned daughter was said to be *epiklēros* ("upon the estate"). The word has sometimes been translated "heiress." "Female orphan" would be an equally good rendering, but "heiress" is acceptable, provided that one recognizes that the woman's rights in the property were limited. Whether she could be said to own the property is perhaps a question of definition; certainly it belonged in law more to her than to her husband, even though as administrator he had a large opportunity to benefit. The main purpose of the institution is disclosed in the provision that her sons should become the owners two years after puberty. The aim was to transmit the inheritance to descendants of the dead man; thus the *oikos* would not become empty. But there was also an aim of providing for the female orphan. An Athenian daughter had a claim on her father's property for her subsistence, and if the woman was not an *epiklēros,* her claim was recognized in the dowry that passed with her on marriage. The similar right of the *epiklēros* was respected in the sole exception to the rule requiring the heir to marry her. If her father died leaving less than a small amount of property, the heir had a choice. He could marry the daughter or he could give her in marriage, provided that he supplied a dowry in an amount determined by his own place in the series of recognized property classes.[30] This exception presumably took care of the case where the father left debts that exceeded his assets. For heirs more remote than begotten or adopted descendants could disclaim the inheritance,[31] but the female orphan had to be provided for.

By the fourth century the Athenians had found a way to avoid the inconveniences created by the rigidity of the rules concerning the *epiklēros.*

---

28. Dem. 57.41; cf. E. Ruschenbusch, "Bemerkungen zum Erbtochterrecht in den solonischen Gesetzen," *Symposion 1988* (Cologne: Böhlau, 1990), 15-19.
29. [Dem.] 46.20; Isai. 8.31; 10.12; Harpok. *epi dietes hēbēsai.*
30. [Dem.] 43.54.
31. [Dem.] 35.3-4; cf. J.H. Lipsius, *Das attische Recht und Rechtsverfahren,* 3 vols. (Leipzig: Reisland, 1905-15), 540-42, 577-79.

The way was adoption and bequest. A woman only became *epiklēros* if her father died leaving no sons. Sons could be begotten or adopted. A man with no begotten sons could adopt a son. So the father of a solitary daughter could adopt a man as his son. But the Athenians imposed a restriction. The father of a solitary daughter could only give or bequeath his property if he also gave his daughter in marriage to the chosen heir.[32] Consequently the purposes of the rules about the *epiklēros* were still achieved within the more flexible practice of adoption and bequest.

The institution of the *epiklēros* is attested in more than one Greek city, although the name varies. It is distinctively Greek. In Rome a person who was *sui iuris* (independent) could own property, whether acquiring it by inheritance or otherwise, and such a person could be male or female. Admittedly a Roman woman required a *tutor* to ratify her transactions, but he was not an administrator of her property. In the pristine form of *tutela legitima,* the *tutor* was the kinsman entitled to inherit from the woman under the rules of intestate succession; his right in relation to her was nothing more than his eventual interest as heir in her property. More will be said in chapter 3 on this matter and on a putative parallel elsewhere.

For the present a concept and an aim call for recognition. The *epiklēros* is an Athenian, perhaps a general Greek, concept. It is rooted in a restriction on female activity. An Athenian woman did not herself carry out major transactions in property. The law provided explicitly that a woman could not perform a transaction in a value exceeding one medimnos of barley.[33] She was restricted to buying and selling on a small scale in retail trade. For dealings in larger value, including dealings in immovable property, she needed a man, called her *kyrios,* as her administrator. Nature often supplied a young woman with a father or brother as her *kyrios*. But if she had no living father or brother, she was an anomaly to Athenian thought. The law stepped in where nature had failed; it provided the woman with a *kyrios* by assigning her in marriage to her nearest male relative. The law of inheritance in general pursued the aim of assigning the rights and obligations of the dead man to an heir. The obligations could include that of providing for a solitary daughter. The institution of the *epiklēros* pursued the aim of providing for the female orphan within the purposive framework set by the general

---

32. Isai. 3.42, 68; 10.13.
33. Isai. 10.10.

law of inheritance. Thus the law had an aim corresponding to the distinctive concept of the *epiklēros*.

The system of law belonging to any community employs concepts proper to that community, and the concepts give rise to corresponding aims. To take an extreme and therefore probatory example, the Greek word *gynē* is translated by the English word "woman." This translation suffices for biology. For comparative law it is inadequate.[34] A woman is a person having the same legal capacities as a man. In private law, for example, she can carry out transactions in property in the same way and under the same restrictions as a man; the transactions include making a will. In public law she can vote, she can hold office, and she can serve as a judge in the same way as a man. An Athenian *gynē* could not do any of the things noted in the last two sentences. The concept of *gynē* in Greek thought was different from the concept of woman, and it generated aims that were accomplished in the distinctive institutions of *kyrieia* and of the *epiklēros*.

It is often possible to discern underlying principles in the law of a community. The word *principle,* though vague, can be serviceable. Sometimes the dangers of vagueness can be escaped if one insists that the underlying things to be sought in the law are concepts and aims. Sometimes indeed principles are preserved by the mere inertia of institutions. An illustration will clarify this point. Let it be supposed that there are two brothers, Otto and Conrad. Their parents have died. Conrad marries and has a son, Henry. Otto remains single and has no children. Otto grows fond of his nephew and makes a will, bequeathing his property to Henry. Henry grows up, pursues an honorable profession, and marries. He and his wife are blessed with a son, Fritz. But disaster strikes the happy relatives. Henry is killed in an automobile accident. Some time later Otto dies without making a new will. Who inherits his property? Systems of the Civil Law and of the Common Law give different answers to this question. In German law, Otto's property goes to Fritz. If Fritz is still a minor, it will be administered for him by a guardian, probably his mother, until he comes of age. In systems of the Common Law, Otto's property passes according to the rules of intestate succession to his nearest surviving relative, that is, to Conrad.

---

34. Cf. R. Just, *Women in Athenian Law and Life* (London: Routledge, 1989), 7-12. Just sets out to discover "the semantic field of 'woman' within the confines of a particular society and culture."

What calls for note is the reason for the difference. German law has inherited principles from Roman law. As noted already, Roman law tried to assign a universal succession to an heir or heirs. Moreover, as will be observed in chapter 3, the most fruitful form of Roman will was an application of a conveyance. When a conveyance transfers ownership of property from one person to another, the rights of the former owner to the property are wholly extinguished. A fortiori, any eventual rights of the former owner's kinsmen to the property are extinguished. Therefore, in the example constructed above, in German law Otto's property became part of Henry's estate when Otto died, and it passed to Henry's heir, Fritz; any rights that Conrad had had to Otto's property were extinguished. But in the Common Law a will merely assigns a specific thing or things to a specific person or persons. If a person to whom a will assigns a thing becomes unable to receive it, for example through death, the will or that part of it cannot take effect.[35] The outcome in German law springs from a Roman principle that is more than two thousand years old. The difference between the Civil Law and the Common Law on this point has nothing to do with current social needs or with any intentions pursued in the twentieth century. The difference in result springs from a difference in the ways in which the Civil Law and the Common Law conceive a will, and the two systems have fashioned and preserved their concepts over a period of many centuries.

Bearing in mind the trio of principles, concepts, and aims, one may return to the aspects of Savigny's theory that provoked this brief survey of selected institutions. That the law can develop without statute is evident from the history of *atimia*. The change in its force came about not by enactment but through practice; the unobtrusive *atimos,* as he may be called, was tolerated. The same conclusion follows from the development of the Athenian will; by the fourth century the restriction that forbade a man to make a will if he had begotten sons could be disregarded, if the testator took enough care to satisfy the interested persons. The history of the *epiklēros* also reveals more change in practice

---

35. For German law on this point see Bähr, *Grundzüge des bürgerlichen Rechts,* 396. On English law see W.W. Buckland and A.D. McNair, *Roman Law and Common Law,* 2d ed. rev. by F.H. Lawson (Cambridge: Cambridge University Press, 1952), 147, 151. If a personal note may be permitted, I made a will while I was writing this essay, and my Californian adviser warned me that, if the person to whom I bequeathed my property predeceased me, the property would pass to my kinsmen in the legal order of intestate succession.

than by statute. Forensic speeches often mention the rules of the institution in hypothetical contexts, but judging from the speeches fathers had learned to prefer adoption or bequest as a way of providing for solitary daughters. Admittedly a statute demanded that the father must give his daughter, together with the inheritance, to the chosen heir.

Pursuing aspects of Savigny's theory further, one should note that developments in the institutions surveyed stayed within recognizable limits or followed discernible lines. *Atimia,* a negative penalty that withdrew protection, continued to be employed and indeed employed widely, even after the state had learned to impose positive penalties of fines, imprisonment, and death. Evidently the Athenians were tolerant in that they were willing to leave some offenders to the mercy of private initiative. Again, the concept of a universal succession guided Roman law to a distinctive result in the case of a will that provided explicitly only for part of the inheritance. It is not known how Athenian law would deal with such an occurrence. But since in Athens bequest to a designated heir amounted to the same as adopting a son, and since sons, begotten or adopted, excluded other relatives, the concept of the *oikos* as the bundle of rights and obligations to be inherited had the same implications as in Rome; in other words, if there was a will designating an heir, the order of succession among relatives more distant than sons played no part. Finally the institution of the *epiklēros* sprang from a distinctive belief about the role of women in relation to property, and the same institution inspired the law that required a testator to give his solitary daughter in marriage to his chosen heir.

Accordingly for Savigny's "nature and character of the nation" one may substitute the trio of principles, concepts, and aims, or one may employ the more romantic expressions, "nature" and "character," if one is willing to give an account of them in terms of that trio. Whichever vocabulary one prefers, one recognizes, thanks to Savigny, that the historical study of law should not restrict itself to discovering rules from historical evidence. Discovery of rules is needed but it is preliminary, and an inquiry that goes no further may be stigmatized as Austinian. Instead of being content with ascertaining rules, the historian should look beneath them for an underlying body of thought. The quest for principles, concepts, and aims is a path toward discovering that body of thought. In larger terms, the task of the historian is to discover how the institution studied fits into the whole body of law current in the given society; or to put the matter yet another way, he must discover how the institution sprang from the way that society conceived the rule of law.³⁶ The meaning of these expressions will perhaps become clearer in subsequent chapters. Meanwhile it is to be noted that the ideas underlying and inspiring the rules and their application are sometimes articulated, especially in a society that has an order of professional and reflective lawyers. In the Greek case the ideas were often latent; patience is required to discover the nature and character of the nation.

It will be appropriate to acknowledge here an aspect of orientation. Concepts, principles, and aims dwell in the human mind. The present essay has been written in the belief that the history of law is a branch not of social but of intellectual history. It has been prompted by the results of a recent study, which found that the lines on which the law develops in a given society are usually determined not by socioeconomic needs but by the normative ideas handed down in that society. When a new predicament requires additional rules, the society tries to elicit them from its legal tradition. Only when the solution to be derived from the legal tradition is considered intolerable does society devise a divergent rule in deference to socioeconomic needs.³⁷ The contrary view, that law

---

36. This program harmonizes (I think) with the idea of "law as integrity," expounded by Dworkin, *Law's Empire*. See for example p. 188: "If people accept that they are governed not only by explicit rules laid down in past political decisions but by whatever other standards flow from the principles that these decisions assume, then the set of recognized public standards can expand and contract organically, as people become more sophisticated in sensing and exploring what these principles require in new circumstances, without the need for detailed legislation or adjudication on each possible point of conflict"; p. 400: "His [the ideal judge's] god is the adjudicative principle, which commands him to see, so far as possible, the law as a coherent and structured whole"; cf. the remarks about "a community of principle" on pp. 211 and 214.

37. Watson, *Evolution*, passim, especially chap. 1. Among arguments offered by Watson for this conclusion two may be called to mind. (1) Romans engaged in exchange by barter from an early date. Indeed coined money was not introduced until ca. 275 B.C. But Roman jurists gave little attention to barter until well into the period of the principate; even then prejustinianic law did not recognize barter as a contract. That is, if a party to an agreed exchange did not deliver, the other party had an action to recover the value of the goods that he had surrendered, not an action to make the defaulter perform his share of the agreement. The offender was regarded as having cheated the other party of some valuables, not as having failed to perform an agreement. For the legal tradition had developed in such a way as to recognize many contracts, but in these performance was either gratuitous or for money. (2) The suit for paternity was denied or provided in geographically adjacent jurisdictions of nineteenth-century Europe. No differences of socioeconomic structure explain the contrast; countries that were homogeneous in society and economy denied or provided the suit because of the historical accident that they had or had not accepted the Napoleonic Code. One may also note the observation in Watson's conclusion (p. 119): "law is largely autonomous and not shaped by societal needs."

develops on lines determined by social and perhaps political factors, is fashionable in some quarters but not easy to defend for private law.[38]

In the spirit outlined in the preceding paragraphs, this essay seeks to discover the Greek concept of justice or law or right. Since the associations of those words can be vague, one may sometimes prefer the expression "the rule of law," which has been employed above. It is used currently without misunderstanding. It is not often defined and it is not easy to define.[39] In simple terms, the rule of law says that people who behave alike are to be treated alike. People should only be treated differently if they have behaved differently. Differences of treatment should be grounded in impersonal distinctions. To determine what "alike" means one must develop substantive and procedural law; one must issue laws and codes; one must interpret, apply, and expound them; there is no end to the enterprise. The rule of law is a goal toward which society may advance; it is still too early in human history to say whether the goal can be wholly achieved. Meanwhile, if like behavior is to receive like treatment, it follows that the rule of law is not restricted to any context of adjudication in courts. If, for example, a parent dies leaving three adult sons or daughters, the rule of law requires equal division between the three survivors, provided that they are alike; it also requires unequal division, if a principle of primogeniture denies that they are alike. Whichever practice is observed, the rule of law can be followed, even though the shares in the inheritance need not be adjudicated by a court.

The expression "the rule of law" will be employed as approximately synonymous with the concept of justice or law or right. The attempt will be made in the ensuing chapters to discern how Greeks came to conceive of society as ordered by the rule of law. Starting from concrete things, chapter 2 will study Greek codes of law in relation to the compilations made by some other nations of antiquity. It will maintain that codes of prescriptive law were a Greek invention. It will also find that

---

38. The view here rejected has been asserted, but not defended in relation to private law, by S. Todd and P. Millett in P. Cartledge, P. Millett, and S. Todd, eds., *Nomos: Essays in Athenian Law, Politics and Society* (Cambridge: Cambridge University Press, 1990), 1–18. See especially p. 10: "law has an organic relationship with its social and political context." In spite of Millett and Todd (p. 6), I have learned to use the expression "private law" of Athens from Dem. 24.192-93.

39. For a discussion of the rule of law see Rawls, *Theory of Justice,* 235-43. One may note here his observation (p. 237): "The rule of law also implies the precept that similar cases be treated similarly."

the Greek codes were understood in a manner different from that in which Romans and modern nations have regarded law. This distinctive manner, being common to many Greek cities, reveals a level of unity in Greek thought. Resuming the theme of unity, chapter 3 will inquire into aspects of substantive law, mainly of the family and of property. The next two chapters will turn from substance to procedure. Chapter 4 will consider how procedures for settling disputes arose among Greeks. In the earliest forms that can be discovered, those procedures were older than the practice of issuing laws in writing, the practice studied in chapter 2. So chapter 4 will attend to ideas preserved in epic verse, it will draw comparisons from other societies, and it will face the question of how compulsory litigation came about. Turning to Athens, where procedure is best attested, chapter 5 will consider magistrates and the development of actions at law.

The final chapter will pay attention to some unfinished business and then it will set off in quest of the original and lasting impulse that prompted Greeks to conceive of law or justice or right. It will maintain that Greeks began from an Indo-European belief in inherent worth, which distinguished each member of the community from all other members, but they proceeded to develop a concept of a community in which a goodly number of men, though distinguished by superiority from the rest of the population, were equal among themselves. They were equal in enjoying the plenitude of privilege, and their equality, realized in substantive and procedural institutions, was the root of the rule of law.

CHAPTER 2

Codes and Compilations of Law

The Lawgivers of Tradition

In the fourth century B.C. people in many parts of Greece believed that the laws of their cities had been issued long before by lawgivers whose names were remembered. The laws of the Cretan cities, for example, had supposedly been issued by the brothers Minos and Rhadamanthys. Minos had learned wisdom from Zeus and had instructed Rhadamanthys, who became a judge and guardian of the laws. The only law of Minos mentioned in this context said that people ought not to drink to the point of intoxication.[1] Stories about Minos have no historical content.

Zaleukos of Italian Lokroi and Charondas of Katane have more chance of being historical. Charondas was said to have made laws for other Greek cities of Sicily and Italy as well as for his own. Aristotle knew their names and that of Philolaos of Corinth, who made laws for the Thebans. But he knew very little about any specific measures of theirs. He said that Charondas had invented the opening step in the lawsuit alleging false testimony; one can only wonder how Aristotle knew.[2] A Greek city suffering internal strife sometimes invited a man or men from another city to come and draw up rules. In this way in the second half of the sixth century, the Parians carried out a settlement at

---

1. Plat. *Min.* 318c-d, 320a-c; *Laws* 624a-b.
2. Ar. *Pol.* 2.1274a22-b8; cf. Plat. *Rep.* 10.599d-e. On the place of this opening step in Athenian practice see Ar. *AP.* 68.4. Material on lawgivers has been collected by M. Gagarin, *Early Greek Law* (Berkeley: University of California Press, 1986), 51-80. The material has been scrutinized for a different purpose by A. Szegedy-Maszak, "Legends of the Greek Lawgivers," *GRBS* 19 (1978): 199-209; discovering a sequence of stock topics, he discerns "the transformation of history by and into myth" (p. 200).

Miletos, and Demonax of Mantinea did so at Kyrene.[3] So it is credible that laws of Charondas were adopted in more than one city of the West. But when the brothel keeper of Herondas (2.48) said that the law read out in court in his case was written by Chairondas [sic], his word was nothing more than proverbial invocation of a great name.

Writing some three hundred years after Aristotle, Diodoros (12.12-21) "knew" far more about Charondas and Zaleukos. He made Charondas a citizen of Thourioi, active some years after the foundation of that city (443). Part of his "information" arose from topics discussed in schools of rhetoric. For example, he credited Charondas with a law that a man who knocked out another man's eye should have one of his own eyes knocked out (12.17). But, Diodoros continued, a man already blind in one eye was threatened, and as the procedure for amendment required, he stood with a noose around his neck and proposed an additional law. Aristotle indicates that in schools of rhetoric there was discussion of the difference between the loss of one eye to a man with two eyes and to a man with only one.[4] Some of the laws attributed by Diodoros to Zaleukos and Charondas were nothing more than witticisms; such, for example, were the "laws" of Zaleukos about errant wives.[5]

Such material is of little value for historical reconstruction, but more can be learned about Diokles, the lawgiver to whom the Syracusans attributed their laws. A statesman of the same name was active in Syracuse late in the fifth century. He proposed severe treatment of the Athenian captives taken in 413 B.C. and later he proposed a change in the constitution with a revision of the laws. So it is easy to understand that Diodoros confused this man with Diokles the lawgiver.[6] But they must be distinguished. The lawgiver was believed to have written a comprehensive code. Later Kephalos in the time of Timoleon (active ca. 345-337 B.C.) and Polydoros in the reign of Hieron (265?-215 B.C.) wrote more laws, but they were both regarded not as lawgivers but as inter-

---

3. Hdt. 5.28-29; 4.161.
4. Ar. *Rhet.* 1.1365b17-19. Demosthenes (24.139-41) told the story of the law and the amendment to entertain his audience; he set it in Lokroi and did not name the lawgiver.
5. Diod. 12.21: a free woman should not be accompanied by more than one maid, unless the free woman was drunk. She should not go out of the city by night, except when she was engaged in an adulterous liaison. She should not wear gold jewelry or a garment with a purple border, unless she was a prostitute. Likewise a husband should not wear a gold-studded ring or a cloak of Milesian type, unless he was on his way to visit a prostitute or commit adultery.
6. Diod. 13.19.4; 13.33.1-13.35.1

preters of the laws of Diokles. The latter's laws were adopted in many cities of Sicily.[7] These features suggest that Diokles the lawgiver was active at a much earlier date than the fifth-century statesman.

This conclusion about date derives some support from the anecdote extant on the content of the laws of Diokles. Allegedly he forbade anyone, under pain of death, to carry a weapon on entering the agora. When the approach of enemies was announced, he went out carrying his sword. But a sudden disturbance in the agora caused him to turn and go thither. Someone reproached him with breaking his own law, but he replied that he upheld it, and he killed himself. The same story is told about Charondas.[8] Evidently it was a theme of folklore that could attach itself to famous names. Possibly the story springs from an early law, adopted in more than one Greek city, to the effect that men must put aside their arms on entering the place of assembly. Such a law may be reflected in the story that at Athens a law of Solon imposed the penalty of *atimia* on anyone who did not stack arms with one side or the other in civil conflict.[9]

At Syracuse there was a temple in honor of Diokles the lawgiver, and he received heroic honors.[10] That is the clue to his identity. Syracuse was a colony of Corinth. Diokles was worshiped in cities near the isthmus. At Megara his tomb was shown and a festival was held in his honor every spring with a competition in kissing. A legend told to explain the tomb said that Diokles had migrated to Megara from Eleusis.[11] Aristophanes (*Acharnians* 774) makes a Megarian swear "by Diokles." The Homeric hymn to Demeter includes Diokles among the lords of Eleusis.[12] A tomb of Diokles was shown at Thebes; Aristotle (*Politics* 2.1274a31-b5) told a romantic story to explain how Diokles arrived there with his lover, Philolaos the lawgiver. Evidently Diokles was not a mortal lawgiver but the recipient of a cult. The settlers at Syracuse brought the cult with them. The laws of the Syracusans, the laws of Diokles, had been issued

---

7. Diod. 13.35; cf. 16.70.7; 16.82.6-7.
8. Diod. 13.33.2-3; 12.19.1-2.
9. Ar. *AP.* 8.5; Plut. *Sol.* 20.1; *Mor.* 550c, 823f; Cic. *Epp. ad Att.* 10.1.2; Gell. *N. A.* 2.12.1. Opinions are collected and doubts expressed by M. Chambers, *Aristoteles Staat der Athener* (Berlin: Akademie Verlag, 1990), 180-81.
10. Diod. 13.35.2. The material of this paragraph is drawn from G. De Sanctis, "Diocle di Siracusa," *Studi italiani di filologia classica* 11 (1903): 433-45.
11. Theokr. 12.27-34, with scholion.
12. *Hymn to Demeter* 153, 474, 477. On the cult of Diokles at Megara see also N.J. Richardson: *The Homeric Hymn to Demeter* (Oxford: Oxford University Press, 1974), 196.

on the authority of the hero (or god). That may explain why Kephalos and Polydoros presented themselves not as novel lawgivers but as interpreters of the laws of Diokles.

The Spartans too claimed to have had an early lawgiver. Herodotos believed that Lykourgos had created "the present order" for them; Xenophon and Aristotle described the institutions of Sparta in some detail and attributed them to Lykourgos.[13] By the time of Plutarch the tradition on him had grown, fostered no doubt by the Spartan reformers of the third century B.C. and later by local guides who conducted Roman tourists. Plutarch credits Lykourgos with the creation of major institutions, such as the *phiditia,* with specific rules, such as prohibition of coinage in gold and silver, and with three so-called *rhētrai.*[14] The abstention from coinage in precious metals may not have sprung from a prohibition; the Spartans simply failed to adopt the new invention when it was spreading among Greek cities in the sixth and fifth centuries B.C. One of the three *rhētrai* calls for note; it forbade the Spartans to have written laws. Thus the Spartans present a paradox; they claimed to have had an early lawgiver but they boasted, truthfully or otherwise, that they had no written laws.

At least the identity of Lykourgos can be ascertained, if one attends to Herodotos. According to the latter, Lykourgos entered the temple at Delphi and the Pythian priestess said that she was more inclined to consider him a god than a man. She was the mouthpiece of Apollo. The Spartans honored Lykourgos as a god with a temple and an annual sacrifice.[15]

Among the traditional lawgivers, some, like Diokles and Lykourgos, were gods or heroes. Others were mortal. The Athenians attributed their laws to Solon, and enough of his poetry is extant to confirm his humanity. But the Athenians attributed their laws on homicide to Drakon, and the hypothesis that those laws were issued on the authority of a sacred snake (*drakōn*) would solve some historical problems.[16] It is impossible to tell whether Charondas, Zaleukos, and Philolaos were mortal or immortal.

---

13. Hdt. 1.65.4-5; Xen. *Lak. Pol.* 1-2; Ar. *Pol.* 2.1270a7, 1271b25, 1273b33, 4.1296a20.
14. Plut. *Lyk.* 9.1; 10.1; 13.1, 3, 5. Much material is collected by D.M. MacDowell, *Spartan Law* (Edinburgh: Scottish Academic Press, 1986).
15. Hdt. 1.65.3; Plut. *Lyk.* 31.4.
16. K.J. Beloch, *Griechische Geschichte* I² (Strassburg: Trübner, 1912), 2.258-62; R. Sealey, *Athenian Republic: Democracy or the Rule of Law?* (University Park: Pennsylvania State University Press, 1987), 115-16.

Timaios of Tauromenion denied the historicity of Zaleukos.[17] The advantage of having an immortal as lawgiver was that laws could be issued on his authority over a period longer than one man's life.

An early lawgiver might be an immortal or a literate mortal. There is even a third possibility. In Sweden, Norway, and Iceland, the earliest compilations of written law were made in the twelfth century A.D. Previously, each community gathered periodically and listened to an officer called "the speaker of the law." He uttered the laws. If the assembled community listened without raising any objection, the laws as uttered remained in force until the next meeting. The names of some such speakers of the law are preserved; they include, for example, in Westgötaland, Lumbaer, the first speaker, and Aeskil Magnusson, the seventeenth, who wrote a book of laws about A.D. 1225.[18] There are no grounds to affirm or deny that this practice or something like it was current in some Greek cities.

At least the North Germanic custom, and the probability that laws attributed to immortal authorities were issued over a protracted period, should prompt the reflection that a Greek city, on adopting the art of writing and applying it to law, did not necessarily move in a single step from a wholly oral procedure to a lengthy compilation of written laws. A city may have written down at first one or a few laws and later a few more, until at last a political crisis prompted issuance of a long collection of laws in writing. This possibility would account for the Athenian tradition that said that annual *thesmothetai* existed before the time of Solon. Aristotle said that the *thesmothetai* were chosen "in order that they should write down the *thesmia* and preserve them with a view to judgment of disputes."[19] He may have derived the purpose from the name, but even if he did, it is not easy to improve on his inference.

The fullest information about Greek compilations of law comes from Athens and from a large inscription found at Gortyn in southern Crete. Before turning to those, it will be proper to consider the ancient codes

---

17. Cic. *de legg.* 2.15.
18. K. von Amira and K.A. Eckhardt, *Germanisches Recht,* 4th ed., 2 vols. (Berlin: de Gruyter, 1960 and 1967), 1:82-88, 98-107, 110-19.
19. Ar. *AP.* 3.4; see the cautious notes of P.J. Rhodes, *A Commentary on the Aristotelian "Athenaion Politeia"* (Oxford: Oxford University Press, 1981), 102-3, and Chambers, *Staat,* 151-52. By the fourth century the function of the *thesmothetai* was care of lawsuits: *AP.* 59. I have not been able to discover whether *thesmia* were the same as *thesmoi* or different. An example of *thesmia* occurs at *AP.* 16.10. *Thesmion* can mean a law (Hdt. 1.59.6; perhaps also Eur. *Tro.* 267) or an *exemplum* (Pind. I. 6.20).

of the Near East with a view to discovering what, if anything, was original in the Greek practice of reducing the law to writing. For the one general certainty about the Greek codes is that they consisted of prescriptive law. That is, their contents were intended to be observed.

The Near Eastern Codes

Excavation and exploration have recovered compilations of laws from Lower Mesopotamia.[20] These belong to two periods, Neo-Sumerian (ca. 2100–ca. 1900 B.C.) and Old Babylonian (ca. 1900–ca. 1595 B.C.). The same two periods have also yielded numerous records of lawsuits.[21] Consideration of Assyrian and Hittite compilations can be postponed until those of Lower Mesopotamia have been considered.

Among the latter the oldest in date of composition is the so-called Laws of Ur-Nammu, who founded the third dynasty of Ur, and is dated 2112–2095 B.C.[22] These laws are known from two copies made in the scribal schools of Nippur and Ur between 1800 and 1700. Parts of a prologue and of some provisions are preserved. The Law-code of Lipit-Ishtar, who probably reigned within the first half of the nineteenth century B.C., is also reconstructed from tablets of clay, seven in number.[23] It has a prologue, a series of provisions of which something like the first half is lost, and an epilogue. The Laws of the City of Eshnunna are

---

20. I rely on the following collections and studies. G.R. Driver and J.C. Miles, *The Babylonian Laws*, 2 vols. (Oxford: Oxford University Press); J.J. Finkelstein, "Ammiṣaduqa's Edict and the Babylonian Law Codes," *Journal of Cuneiform Studies* 15 (1961): 91–104; J.J. Finkelstein, "Sex Offences in Sumerian Laws," *Journal of the American Oriental Society* 86 (1966): 355–72.; N. Yoffee, "Context and authority in early Mesopotamian law," in R. Cohen and J.D. Toland, eds., *State Formation and Political Legitimacy* (Political Anthropology 6, New Brunswick and Oxford, 1988), 95–113; cf. J.B. Pritchard, *Ancient Near Eastern Texts Relating to the Old Testament*, 3d ed. (Princeton: Princeton University Press, 1969), 159–80, 523–28. I thank Mr. M.F. Ierardi for drawing my attention to Finkelstein's influential article of 1961. I also thank Professor N. Yoffee for giving me a copy of his article and telling me that the Laws of Ur-Nammu should now be ascribed to his son, Shulgi. I am indebted essentially to Finkelstein for my understanding of the codes. His findings are known to Assyriologists but as yet not to many Hellenists; it is to be hoped that his work will become acknowledged more widely.

21. I rely on the following works: A. Walther, *Das altbabylonische Gerichtswesen* (Leipzig: Hinrichs, 1917); J.G. Lautner, *Die richterliche Entscheidung und die Streitbeendigung im altbabylonischen Prozessrechte* (Leipzig: Weicher, 1922); A. Falkenstein, *Die neusumerischen Gerichtsurkunden I* (Munich: Bayerische Akademie der Wissenschaften, 1956).

22. Pritchard, *Ancient Near Eastern Texts*, 523–25.

23. Ibid., 159–61.

known from two tablets found near Baghdad.[24] The extant text consists of sixty-one rules. Its place in the historical development is not clear. The most imposing compilation is the Code of Hammurapi, who may have reigned from 1728 to 1686 B.C.[25] It was inscribed on a large stele of diorite. A bas-relief surmounting the text shows the god Shamash commissioning Hammurapi to write laws. The text consists of a prologue, a list of provisions, and an epilogue. Both the prologue and the epilogue are long and semipoetic in style. Later, probably in the twelfth century, Elamite raiders carried off the stele and set it up in Susa, their capital. French archaeologists found it in A.D. 1901-2 and took it to the Louvre. A considerable part of the provisions (paragraphs 65-100, out of the total of 282) had been chiseled off by the Elamites but can be restored from copies on tablets of clay.

The codes must be distinguished from royal utterances of another kind, called *misharum*-acts. These latter are well represented by the edict of Ammiṣaduqa, who reigned 1646-1626 B.C.[26] Although the opening and end of this text are lost, it cannot have had an elaborate prologue or epilogue, such as characterize the law-codes. It may have opened by stating its royal source of authority and ended with a scribe's note, perhaps giving a date. A *misharum*-act was often issued at the beginning of the reign, but some were issued at a later date. It was a temporary remission of debts and other obligations and it provided for the reversion of holdings of land to their original owners. It sought thus to restore an equilibrium that had been disturbed. It had a real effect on economic activity.

The law-codes, on the other hand, were issued late in the reign of each king. The prologue proclaimed the king's achievements. Lipit-Ishtar said that the gods Anu and Enlil had called him to rule Sumer and Akkad, that he had overcome rebellion and enmity and established justice, that he had made the father support the children and the children support the father. The prologue of Hammurapi began by naming the gods who had set him to uphold justice and foster prosperity; it recounted his achievements in building temples, winning wars, and bringing

---

24. Ibid., 161-63.
25. Ibid., 163-80.
26. Ibid., 526-28; cf. Finkelstein, "Ammiṣaduqa's Edict." Understanding of *misharum*-acts has been improved by F.R. Kraus, "Ein Edikt des Königs Samsu-iluna von Babylon," *Assyriological Studies* 16 (1965): 225-31, and J.J. Finkelstein, "Some New *Misharum* Material and Its Implications," *Assyriological Studies* 16 (1965): 233-46.

prosperity to the cities. Ur-Nammu (or rather Shulgi, see n. 20) claimed in his prologue to have protected orphans and widows in addition to standardizing weights. Likewise in the epilogues, the kings claim to have established justice, abolished enmity and rebellion, and brought prosperity to their subjects. Lipit-Ishtar and Hammurapi each conclude by mentioning the stele on which his laws are now inscribed and cursing anyone who damages it.

Neither in the prologues nor in the epilogues nor elsewhere do the law-codes order anyone to observe their provisions. Judgments in lawsuits pay no regard to the law-codes.[27] They did not incorporate the primary ingredient of a *misharum*-act, namely a temporary remission of financial obligations. They were "pious hopes and moral resolve rather than effective law."[28] They were "royal apologia and testaments. Their primary purpose was to lay before the public, posterity, future kings, and, above all, the gods, evidence of the king's execution of his divinely ordained mandate."[29]

The codes could accordingly pass into the traditional body of literature that served to train scribes.[30] Hence they were copied on tablets of clay at dates long after the deaths of the kings who had issued them. Similarities in content of the codes arise, not from continued application of legal principles in transactions or adjudication, but from a literary tradition. A fragmentary tablet gives part of a student's exercise of about 1800 B.C.[31] Like the provisions of the codes, the formulation is casuistic; that is, each paragraph begins with a hypothetical occurrence introduced with a word equivalent to *if*. Comparison of the fragment with provisions on sexual offenses in the codes has shown that the compilers did not try to offer a practical guide for judges. Such a guide would need to distinguish different elements of the occurrence, as these told in favor of one or the other party to a dispute. When a case goes to court, it is usually complex; that is, each of the two parties can assert things which

---

27. Walther, *Altbabylonisches Gerichtswesen,* 227. In Neo-Sumerian records the reasons for the judgment are sometimes given but they are always the facts of the case, never a law (Falkenstein, *Neusumerischen Gerichtsurkunden,* 76–77); see chapter 6, "Mesopotamian justice."

28. Finkelstein, "Ammiṣaduqa's Edict," 102.

29. Ibid., 103.

30. A. Leo Oppenheim: *Ancient Mesopotamia* (Chicago: University of Chicago Press, 1964), 12–21.

31. *YBT* I, 28 (*YBC* 2177 in Pritchard 525–26), elucidated by Finkelstein, "Sex Offences," 357–66.

tell in his own favor (if the case were simple, if all the circumstances favored one party, there would be a good chance of reaching a settlement out of court). To be serviceable, a handbook for judges must outline the types of circumstance that each party may allege and it must tell the judge what weight to attach to each circumstance. But in the Mesopotamian codes each hypothetical situation is constructed to point in only one direction to a judgment. "These documents were not designed as exercises in legal casuistry, but as exemplifications of the meting out of justice."[32]

The conclusion to be drawn is that the so-called law-codes of Lower Mesopotamia do not consist of prescriptive rules. A *misharum*-act was indeed prescriptive, but it did not have the permanent validity of a law; it was temporary in effect and was intended to be temporary. On the other hand a royal code was a display of the king's moral quality as a just ruler, proclaiming himself to the gods, even though the code might incorporate material drawn ultimately from a *misharum*-act and it might bear some relation to law as observed in transactions and judgments. Such a code could easily pass into the traditional material of the scribal schools; from the material the scribes learned the arts of writing and phrasing with a view to their subsequent employment as diviners and exorcists. Copied onto tablets of clay, the codes were not legal but literary in character.

The Assyrian material is less plentiful and more difficult to diagnose.[33] There are two groups of tablets. First, the Old Assyrian Laws consist of three tablets, poorly preserved. They probably come not from the capital city of Aššur but from a trading colony of the Assyrians in Asia Minor, and they belong within the Old Assyrian period, ca. 2350-ca. 2100 B.C. They appear to give "the arrangements for the session of the commercial court of the community,"[34] but they are too fragmentary to allow any firm inference.

The other group of texts, the Middle Assyrian Laws, is rather more promising. It consists of ten or eleven tablets (eleven pieces, but two of them are parts of a single tablet). They come from Aššur and belong to the period ca. 1450-ca. 1250 B.C. Differences of orthography and

---

32. Finkelstein, "Sex Offences," 368.
33. Driver and Miles, *Assyrian Laws;* also Pritchard, *Ancient Near Eastern Texts* 180-88 (the Middle Assyrian laws). Some useful comments on marriage and bride-price in the Middle Assyrian laws are provided by P. Cruveilhier, "Le lévirat chez les Hébreux et chez les Assyriens," *Revue Biblique* 34 (1925): 524-46.
34. Driver and Miles, *Assyrian Laws,* 3.

grammatical form show that the tablets vary in date, though not widely. Most of them are poorly preserved fragments. Three of them are in rather better condition, and one of these, Tablet A, is well preserved. Any judgment on the character of the documents has to rely on Tablet A.

This tablet consists of fifty-nine sections. Most of them deal with women. There are provisions about offenses committed by women and about offenses committed against women. There are rules about adultery and (secs. 30, 31) about betrothal gifts or bride-price. Some sections deal with the ornaments of a widow given to her by her husband (26), with the inheritance of a child of a woman who married twice (28), and with the classes of women who may or may not wear veils (38). In some provisions the occurrence of women is incidental; section 47 orders the penalty of death if a man or a woman makes magical preparations. In others it is remote; section 18 penalizes a man who says falsely to his neighbor that men have committed adultery with the neighbor's wife. Occasionally women are absent; section 20 imposes a penalty for sodomy of a male partner, and section 19 says what is to be done if a man spreads a rumor against another man by saying that men have taken him as a homosexual partner.

The editors considered two hypotheses about the character of this miscellaneous collection.[35] The one was that it is not the work of a lawgiver but of a jurist, a private person, who drew on earlier compilations by jurists as well as on enactments. But the contents of the tablet are too disparate for it to serve as a practical handbook for someone administering the law. Likewise it lacks any orderly arrangement such as should be expected in a work designed to instruct students of law. The editors themselves preferred the hypothesis that the tablet is the work of a legislator who set out to amend the law; that is, it presupposes a current body of law concerning women and it carries out reforms. Against this hypothesis it must be objected that the supposed reforms are an amazingly confused and lengthy collection.

The editors assumed that the tablets consist essentially of legal material. They were at work before Finkelstein's study showed that other things may be present in a list of provisions in cuneiform. The tentative hypothesis should be that Tablet A and the Middle Assyrian Laws in general are not legal but literary. They have a place within the libraries where scribes learned their art. They may bear some relation to law, but

---

35. Ibid., 12-15.

the relationship is remote. It is probably fair to conclude from Tablet A, for example, that betrothal gifts were made, that sodomy and sorcery incurred disapproval, and that some women wore veils. But it would be hazardous to infer anything more precise about life as distinct from literature.

The texts called "the Hittite Laws" allow firmer conclusions.[36] There are two texts, each preserved in several copies on tablets of clay. The one text begins with the words "If a man" and ends with a scribal subscription or colophon, which calls the text "If a man." The other text begins with the words "If a vine" and is so called in the scribal colophon at the end. Study of the language, script, and material content of the tablets shows that the texts developed over a long period. Many of the extant copies of "If a man" were made in the thirteenth century B.C. but they are based on an earlier text from the middle of the fifteenth century or still earlier (Kammenhuber, 77-82). The mutual relation between the copies of "If a vine" is complex; the tablets are not the product of a single line of transmission (127). Study of the penalties provided in the rules suggests that they have developed over a period of half a millennium or more; mutilations are mentioned but have been superseded by payments in valuables; these in turn have decreased, but at the end of the development the last clauses of "If a vine" impose the death penalty for moral offenses (Korošec).

To a large extent the material is arranged in an orderly manner. Thus "If a man" begins with the law of persons (secs. 1-56), continues with property in animals (57-92), and concludes with property in buildings (93-100; cf. Korošec, 121-24). So its later part is much concerned with theft. "If a vine" begins with theft from fruit trees and proceeds to other agricultural produce and agrarian equipment. The two texts complement one another. They may be closely related to practical administration of law.

A clue toward understanding the texts can be drawn from provisions that tell of a decrease in penalty. For example, section 9 of "If a man" says what is to be done if someone has injured someone else in the head.

---

36. References will be given by name of author. The basic work is Friedrich: *Die hethitischen Gesetze* (Leiden: Brill, 1959). It was reviewed by A. Kammenhuber, *Bibliotheca Orientalis* 18 (1961): 77-82, cf. 124-27, and by H.G. Güterbock, *Journal of Cuneiform Studies* 15 (1961): 62-78, cf. 16 (1962): 17-23. For the texts, see also Pritchard, *Ancient Near Eastern Texts,* 188-97. There is a valuable study: V. Korošec, "Les lois hittites et leur évolution," *Revue d' Assyriologie et d' Archéologie Orientale* 57 (1963): 121-44.

Previously the aggressor paid six shekels, of which the victim took three and the palace took the other three shekels; but now the king has abolished the payment due to the palace, and so the aggressor pays only the three shekels due to the victim. Again, section 25 of the same text, though less well preserved, deals with the offense of soiling a vessel or a source of water. Previously the offender paid a total amount (not preserved) and the palace took three shekels of this; now the king has abolished the payment due to the palace and the offender pays only three (?) shekels to the person whose interests have been harmed. Korošec (128–36) noted about twenty provisions that mention a decrease in penalty on these lines; he supposed that a single king had carried out an extensive reform. That may be so, although there is no apparent objection to the other possibility that a series of kings had diminished penalties piecemeal. Oriental monarchs often had a prerogative of remitting obligations and exercised it as a gesture of clemency. The salient fact in the provisions reporting decrease in penalties is that the king is spoken of in the third person and his name is not given. So the Hittite Laws differ from some other compilations of the ancient Near East. The probable inference to be drawn is that the author of the texts is a person (or persons) other than the king.

The easiest hypothesis about the character of the two texts is that each is a "book of law," compiled by a private person or persons who had knowledge and experience of legal activities, intended to assist administrators, judges, perhaps students bent on becoming administrators or judges, and perhaps private persons engaging in transactions. Such a book of law is often called a *Rechtsbuch* or *Landrechtsbuch* after the model of the *Sachsenspiegel* and other mediaeval compilations.[37] One may call the author of a book of law a jurist. He does not exercise public authority and his book does not have the force of legislation. His primary aim in writing his book is not to reform the law but to expound it as it is. Yet in expounding the law he tries to achieve clarity, and the attempt to clarify may come close to developing the law by interpretation.

If this way of understanding the Hittite Laws is right, they are markedly different from the Mesopotamian and Assyrian "laws." On the other hand they are not strictly prescriptive codes. The jurists who compiled

---

37. See chap. 1 at n. 15 for the meaning intended by the phrase "book of law." A book of law has rather less authority than the (few) "books of authority" recognized in English law (on them see D. Henrich, *Einführung in das englische Privatrecht,* 2d ed. [Darmstadt: Wissenschaftliche Buchgesellschaft, 1993], 24–25).

them did not give them authority; any authority inherent in the provisions derived from the institutions that the compilers tried to describe. Yet the Hittite Laws, thus understood, are on the threshold that leads to prescriptive rules. The Greeks crossed that threshold.

Gortyn

Thanks to the recovery between A.D. 1857 and 1884 of a handsome inscription, the laws of Gortyn in southern Crete are better known in one respect than those of any other Greek city of antiquity.[38] The inscription was cut in twelve columns on an arc of a circular wall; the arc was about nine meters long, and if the circle was completed, it had a diameter of about thirty meters. The wall had originally been erected as part of a building, perhaps a court of law. Later, in the Roman period, it was dismantled and set up afresh at a new site to support a theater.

The number of inscribed lines varies between 53 and 56 in each of the first eleven columns. The twelfth column ends in its nineteenth line. Like many decrees of Greek cities, the inscription begins with the word "Gods," the four letters being spread to occupy the whole of the first line; possibly this device indicated the authoritative character of the provisions. The beginning and end of the inscription are thus preserved. There is a lacuna of nearly fourteen lines at the top of column X. Parts of the last lines of columns IV, VI, VII, and VIII have been lost. Otherwise, apart from some small lacunas, by far the greater part of the text is readily legible. The last part, starting at column XI, line 24, is in a different hand. It can well be called "Additional laws," since at least some of its provisions supplement those in the main part of the text. There is also another Gortynian inscription, sometimes called "The Second Code" (*Inscriptiones Creticae* IV, 41). It consists of seven inscribed columns, and these vary in length between sixteen and nineteen lines. It has provisions on damage by farm animals, on misappropriation of domesticated animals and birds, on the slave who takes refuge in a sanctuary, and on the man who has pledged his person as security for a loan.

---

38. M. Guarducci (*Inscriptiones Creticae* IV, 72) provides a text with photographs and a facsimile, a Latin translation, and a commentary. R.F. Willetts, *The Law Code of Gortyn* (Berlin: de Gruyter, 1967), provides an introduction, a text with Guarducci's facsimile, an English translation, and a commentary; his philological explanations are useful, but on other matters see the important review by H. Meyer-Laurin in *Gnomon* 41 (1969): 160–65.

It is often supposed, because of the manner of inscribing (*boustrophēdon*) and the forms of the letters, that the inscription was cut in the fifth century.[39] Most of what little is known about the development of the Cretan alphabet depends on coins, and the difference in the medium adds to the uncertainty of the inference. Dates in the sixth and fourth centuries cannot be excluded. At least, if the inscription had been cut in the third century or later, one would expect to detect the influence of *koinē* Greek.

There are further uncertainties. Nothing is known about the occasion that caused someone to inscribe the code: was there a political conflict? The relation of the main text to the additional laws, and of the whole to the Second Code, is obscure. It is difficult to tell how far the provisions are traditional and how far innovatory. Some of them are accompanied by a prohibition of retroactive enforcement (V, 1-9; VI, 9-25; XII, 1-5); some degree of innovation is implied, but one may wonder, how much.

It is easy to recognize systematic classification of material in most of the code. After an opening section (I, 2 to II, 2), which will require attention shortly, there are provisions about sexual offenses (II, 2-45). These are followed by rules about dissolution of marriage by divorce or death of one party (II, 45 to IV, 23). Next come rules on inheritance (IV, 23 to VI, 2), and these are followed by provisions protecting the separate property of different members of the family (VI, 2-46). The short provisions following are somewhat miscellaneous, for they deal with ransom (VI, 46-56), with mixed marriages between free and unfree persons (VI, 56 to VII, 10), and with purchase of slaves (VII, 10-15). After these there follows a long and readily distinguishable section on the heiress or female orphan (VII, 15 to IX, 24). Next there are, again, somewhat miscellaneous provisions about deceased debtors, sureties, and various gifts and debts (IX, 24 to X, 32). The main text closes with a relatively short but coherent section on adoption (X, 33 to XI, 23), and this is followed by the additional laws (XI, 24 to XII, 19).

The meaning of the first law in the code has lately been disputed. An understanding of this law may clarify the character of the code as a whole. The first section (I, 2 to II, 2) deals with seizures and concludes by saying that one may seize a man with impunity after he has been

---

39. M. Guarducci ("Intorno alle vicende e all' età della grande iscrizione di Gortina," *RFIC*, n.s., 16 [1938]: 264-73) attempted a more precise date.

defeated in a lawsuit or has pledged his person as security (I, 56 to II, 2). The preceding provisions mostly forbid seizures and say what remedial action is to be taken if a forbidden seizure has been made. The first law has been rendered in two contrasting ways:

1. Whoever prepares to contend at law about a free man or a slave, let him not make a seizure before trial
2. Whoever prepares to contend at law against a free man or a slave, let him not make a seizure before trial.[40]

There are strong arguments of philology in favor of the first rendering, but some difficulties of substance require attention, because their solution may help toward further understanding of the laws. Against the second reading it can be urged that slaves are not otherwise known to have appeared as parties in lawsuits at Gortyn. In reply it can be observed that "slave" in the expression "a free man or a slave" includes all unfree persons, and these were of more than one kind. Apart from the chattel slave, who could be bought in the market (VII, 10-15), there was the agrarian serf (*woikeus*). The latter is said to have farm animals, and the house in which he dwells is exempted from the general rules distributing the property of a free man at death to his sons (IV, 31-43), again, if a male and female serf are separated, there are provisions for distributing property between them (III, 40-44). It seems to follow that an agrarian serf could in some sense own property; if so, it is likely that he could engage in litigation.

An objection of content to the first rendering may lead further. That rendering envisages two men who have a dispute "about a free man or a slave." It is easy to see how a dispute might arise about a slave; two free men might each believe that they owned the same slave. But it is not clear how a dispute could arise in the same sense about a free man.

---

40. The second rendering ("against") was proposed by H.B. Rosén ("Questions d' interprétation de textes juridiques grecs de la plus ancienne époque," *Symposion 1977* [Cologne: Böhlau, 1982], 9-32) and defended by H. van Effenterre ("Le droit et la langue à propos du code de Gortyne," *Symposion 1979* [Cologne: Böhlau, 1983], 115-28, and "Problèmes d' épigraphie juridique. A propos d' un livre d' Alberto Maffi," *Revue Historique de Droit français et étranger* 62 [1984]: 47-52). The first rendering, which is older, has been defended by A. Maffi (*Studi di epigrafia giuridica greca* [Milano: Giuffre, 1983], 3-117) and M. Gagarin ("The First Law of the Gortyn Code," *GRBS* 29 [1988]: 335-43). Gagarin's presentation of the philological arguments is cogent and need not be repeated here.

Toward meeting this difficulty one may pay attention to the apodosis of the first law, which has had less discussion of late than the protasis. The law forbids a disputant to make a seizure before trial but does not say what is (not) to be seized. There are three possibilities:

a) The party is forbidden to seize the thing at issue between him and his adversary. This interpretation makes good sense of a dispute about a slave, but a free man is not likely to be the thing in dispute between two adversaries.
b) The party is forbidden to seize his adversary. That is, he is forbidden to carry out an act of self-help with a view to compelling his adversary to surrender the thing in dispute.
c) Both prohibitions are intended. For if a party had recourse to self-help, he might try to put his adversary under constraint by seizing the adversary or by seizing property, such as a slave, that belonged to the adversary.

Interpretations *b* and *c* make sense of the reference to a free man in the protasis, "Whoever prepares to contend at law about a free man or a slave." For the law envisages the risk that a party may seize his adversary before trial; then the other party will be both adversary and subject of the dispute. Moreover, both interpretations make good sense of the last law in the first section of the code. That last law (I, 56 to II, 2) says that one may seize with impunity a man who has been defeated in a lawsuit or has pledged his person as security. Not much can be said about the man who has pledged his person as security, since little is known about Gortynian procedures of surety. But permission to seize a defeated litigant can well close the section on seizures. In Roman terms, the first law (I, 2–3) forbids *pignoris capio* and *manus iniectio* before trial, but the last law of the section (I, 56 to II, 2) allows *manus iniectio* as a mode of execution after judgment has been given. The intervening laws of the first section are in harmony with this understanding.

It follows that the first section (I, 2 to II, 2) is not laws on the particular matter of disputed rights over free men and slaves. It is a general prohibition against self-help before recourse to forensic justice. Therefore its place at the beginning of the code is appropriate on grounds of jurisprudence. A detached contemplation of law can well begin by recognizing the fundamental choice between self-help and judicial litigation. So the code as a whole is not a mere list of rules arranged according to subject matter. Even though political conflicts may have contributed to formulating the laws in part, the code was the product of a process of thought in which disinterested inquiry played a significant role.

Parts of the code will be noted in later chapters. Three further general features call for attention here. The first concerns the tasks assigned to judges. The judge is always spoken of in the singular and he performs tasks of two kinds. They are distinguished in one of the additional laws (XI, 26-31). On the one hand there are matters on which the laws provide that the testimony of witnesses or a sworn declaration by a party is to be decisive, and on these the judge is merely to issue an order on the basis of the testimony or declaration. But on other matters he is himself to swear an oath and make a determination in the light of the contentions. The laws provide plentiful illustrations of both tasks.[41] Thus it is assumed that the laws, authorizing sworn assertions by witnesses or parties, have provided in advance the solutions to some predicaments, but other predicaments arise and the judge has discretionary authority to decide these. A comparable distinction in the tasks of the judge and a comparable conception of the function of the laws will be recognized shortly in Athens and other cities.

A second general feature concerns offenses. The laws mention some misdeeds that can be called "fraud," although the laws do not give them any common name or classification. For example, a husband is not to sell or mortgage property of his wife, and a son is not to sell or mortgage property of his mother. If a man alienates property of his wife or mother in contravention of this rule, the property is to be restored to the woman; the man who alienated it is to pay twice its value to the man who acquired it and shall make good any loss he has caused (VI, 9-24). Again, a widowed father is not to sell or mortgage property of his children, unless they are of full age and have given their consent. If the father alienates their property in contravention of this prohibition, the property is to be restored to the children; the man who alienated it is to pay twice its value to the man who acquired it and shall make good any loss he has caused (VI, 31-44). Likewise, if a man at death owes a debt and leaves a daughter but no sons, the daughter may in person, or through the

---

41. The testimony of witnesses is decisive at I, 20-21; II, 15-16; III, 49-52; IX, 29-37. The oath of a party is decisive at III, 5-12; XI, 46-50; probably also at IX, 54. Passages requiring the judge to make a determination on oath include I, 11-12; I, 13-14; I, 23-24; II, 54 to III, 1; VI, 51-55.

agency of her relatives, sell or mortgage property to the extent required to pay off the debt. But if anyone sells or mortgages the property beyond this limit, the property is to be restored to the heiress; the man who alienated it is to pay twice its value to the man who acquired it and shall make good any loss he has caused (IX, 1-15). In each of these passages the offense consists in alienation of property by someone who was not the owner. He is held to have committed an offense against the person to whom he alienated it. The salient point is that the punitive payment in twice the value of the property is to be made to the person against whom the offense was committed. A general consideration must be noticed here in explanation.

If one person inflicts harm of any kind on another person, the misdeed has different aspects. There is, first, the aspect of loss and compensation. Many systems of law, ancient and modern, recognize the victim's right to compensation for the economic loss he has sustained, and so they allow him a civil action.

A second aspect, which receives plentiful attention in modern systems, is that of crime. When an offender inflicts harm, such as theft, bodily injury, or death, the deed is held to harm the whole community because it disturbs the peace. So legal proceedings against the offender are undertaken by a public prosecutor, who represents the king or queen, or, in countries that no longer have a monarch, an abstraction called the state, which has replaced the monarch. The victim of the offense serves not as a party to the lawsuit but as a witness. If the punishment is a fine, it is paid to the state or the king, not to the victim. Criminal proceedings arose from the ambitions of mediaeval kings, who claimed to maintain the peace and treated the harm inflicted by one subject on another as an affront to the royal majesty. The sphere in which the king maintained the peace was the whole land that he ruled. Criminal proceedings are preserved by a legal fiction, which treats the infliction of harm on a single person as if it harmed or threatened the welfare of the community.

A misdeed has yet a third aspect, one which receives little or no attention in modern systems but was prominent in Roman law and in the law of some other ancient communities. The misdeed is an affront to the majesty of the private person who is its victim. It disturbs the peace in the sphere where he exercises authority; it may, for example, inflict bodily injury on him or challenge his rule over his own household. If the misdeed goes unpunished or unavenged, the victim's standing in society is diminished. To restore the victim's standing the aggressor must make a payment in valuables to him. This aspect of the misdeed is called delict, and the payment can be called a delictal payment.[42] This payment is separate from compensation for loss. The provisions, reviewed above, about fraud in the laws of Gortyn require the offender to make good any loss he has caused in addition to paying a delictal payment in twice the value of the thing he had wrongfully alienated. The laws of Gortyn recognize delict; they do not include a concept of crime. In a later chapter (5) the question will be asked, whether Athenian law recognized crime as well as delict.

It remains thirdly and finally to note that nearly all of the laws inscribed at Gortyn are casuistic in formulation. That is, they begin with a protasis in the form, "If someone does such and such a thing" or "Whoever does such and such a thing," and they continue with an apodosis stating a remedy. This formulation may reflect a condition where previously particular cases were determined at the judge's discretion but became the models for generalizations. This possibility should not be forgotten in approaching the Athenian codes.

Athens

Athenians of the classical period said that their laws had been made for them long before by Solon. Herodotos said that Solon had made laws (*nomoi*) for the Athenians at their bidding, and in an extant poem, giving an account of his public work, Solon said that he had written laws (*thesmoi*).[43] The classical Athenians also attributed their laws on homicide to Drakon. To solve the historical problem posed by the rival claims of the two lawgivers, Aristotle supposed that Drakon had written laws extensively and Solon repealed all of them except the ones on homicide. This explanation is rationalistic in the spirit of fourth-century speculation. It is also inadequate; it does not explain what merit brought about the preservation of Drakon's laws on homicide and why his other laws lacked that merit.[44] The hard data remain that the Athenians attributed their laws to Solon and their laws on homicide to Drakon.

---

42. On the concept of delict one may consult handbooks of Roman law, for example B. Nicholas, *An Introduction to Roman Law* (Oxford: Oxford University Press, 1962), 207-9; R.W. Leage, *Roman Private Law,* 3d ed. (London: Macmillan, 1961), 394-97.

43. Hdt. 1.29.1; Solon fr. 36 (West), apud Ar. *AP.* 12.4, lines 18-20.

44. Ar. *AP.* 4.1; 7.1. The hypothesis that Drakon made laws on subjects other than homicide is defended by R.S. Stroud, *Drakon's Law on Homicide* (Berkeley: University

The Athenians distinguished between laws of two kinds: those that regulate relations between citizens and those that regulate the relation of each citizen to the community.[45] This is the distinction between private and public law. It deserves to be drawn, even though the one branch could impinge on the other as soon as there were public officers to uphold private law. Most of the changes scrutinized in studies of Athenian constitutional history belonged to public law. Likewise most of the known decrees passed by the Athenians in the fifth century dealt with policy of the state. There is little direct information about changes in private law; one notices the measure of 451/0 B.C. restricting citizenship to children whose parents were both citizens.[46] The sharp growth of population and prosperity in the period of the Delian League must have raised plentiful new questions in relations between persons, that is, it must have created a need for enlarging the body of private law; one cannot tell how that need was met.

In the later part of the fifth century, the Athenians set about revising their laws. After reversing the revolution of 411, they appointed lawgivers (*nomothetai*). In 409/8 B.C. officers called "recorders [*anagrapheis*] of the laws" had a document entitled "the law [*nomos*] of Drakon on homicide" inscribed on stone. A certain Nikomachos served as recorder of laws, whether on this board or another, for six years, ending with the defeat of Athens in the Peloponnesian War.[47] Evidently a good deal of thought was being given to reform of the laws. There is no need to assume that the attested boards were the only ones in action or that the work had not begun before the earliest attested date.

Work was interrupted by the siege and surrender of Athens. Soon afterwards the Thirty were installed; they were authorized to write laws and to exercise control of the city in the meantime. They carried out some changes in private law, for example in the law of bequest, but they devoted more energy to the other part of their task.[48] After they had

---

of California Press, 1968), 77–82. For a different view see Sealey, *Athenian Republic,* 115–16.

45. Dem. 24.192–93. For the modern distinction between public and private law see, for example, P. Bähr, *Grundzüge des bürgerlichen Rechts,* 7th ed. (Munich: Vahlen, 1989), 10–12.

46. Ar. *AP.* 26.4; studied by C. Patterson, *Pericles' Citizenship Law of 451–50 B.C.* (New York: Arno Press, 1981).

47. Thuc. 8.97.2; *IG* I³, 104 = Meiggs and Lewis no. 86; Lys. 30.2. The possible relation between the variously attested boards is discussed by Stroud, *Drakon's Law,* 22–24.

48. Xen. *Hell.* 2.3.2 and 11; Ar. *AP.* 35.2.

been overthrown, the Athenians set about revising their laws thoroughly. Andokides (1.82-89) preserves one of the decrees, a decree proposed by Teisamenos, which launched the work of revision, and he cites five further measures passed at this time to determine what should be valid law henceforth. Nikomachos served again as a recorder of laws. When his task had been completed, he was prosecuted on a charge concerning sacrifices included in the revised calendar or omitted from it. A speech for the prosecution has been preserved in the corpus attributed to Lysias and says that Nikomachos served this time for four years (30.4). It appears to follow that in the course of the four Attic years 403/2-400/399 B.C. the laws were revised and the result was a new code. But lately this conclusion has been challenged.[49] The reasons require attention.

One may start from the decree of Teisamenos. It reads thus:

> Resolved by the demos, on the proposal of Teisamenos: let the Athenians conduct their affairs in accordance with ancestral practice. Let them observe the laws [*nomoi*] of Solon and his measures and weights, and let them observe the laws [*thesmoi*] of Drakon, as we observed them in the previous period. Wherever additional laws are needed, let those lawgivers [*nomothetai*] who have been chosen by the council write proposals down and set them up beside the statues of the eponymous heroes for anyone who wishes to inspect, and let them hand them over to the magistracies [*archai*] in the present month. But let the laws [*nomoi*] that are handed over be ratified by scrutiny beforehand by the council and the five hundred lawgivers [*nomothetai*], who have been chosen by their fellow demesmen, after they have sworn an oath. Let any private person who wishes be permitted to go into the council and give any good advice he has about the laws [*nomoi*]. When the laws have been made, let the council of the Areopagos take care of the laws [*nomoi*], so that the magistracies observe the current laws [*hoi keimenoi nomoi*]. Let those of the laws that are validated be inscribed on the wall, where they were previously inscribed, for anyone who wishes to inspect.[50]

---

49. N. Robertson, "The Laws of Athens, 410-399: The Evidence for Review and Publication," *JHS* 110 (1990): 43-75. P.J. Rhodes, "The Athenian Code of Laws, 410-399 B.C.," *JHS* 111 (1991): 87-100, diverges from Robertson and offers a comprehensive account, with which I am mostly in agreement.

50. Andok. 1.83-84. The word *nomos* is used both for a measure that has been brought into force (an act) and for a proposal on which a decision is still to be taken (a bill). The same variation is illustrated by Dem. 20.89-90, 94-95, 97-101; 24.23, 25-26, 32-34.

The last sentence must be quoted, since its meaning has been disputed.

τοὺς δὲ κυρουμένους τῶν νόμων ἀναγράφειν εἰς τὸν τοῖχον, ἵνα περ πρότερον ἀνεγράφησαν, σκοπεῖν τῶι βουλομένωι.

Some recent readers have noticed that the participle (*kyroumenous*) is present. So it differs from the aorist participle employed by Andokides, when he resumes speaking after the decree has been read out:

> So the laws were ratified by scrutiny, gentlemen, in accordance with this decree, and they inscribed the validated laws [*tous kyrōthentas*] in the stoa. (1.85)

The recent readers have concluded that the texts to be inscribed on the wall were not the laws that had been validated but the bills under consideration for possible ratification.[51]

This inference drawn from the tense of the participle does not follow. A present participle can refer to time that is past in relation to that of the finite verb. Thus Thucydides wrote:

> It appears that the land now called Hellas was not of old securely inhabited.
>
> [φαίνεται γὰρ ἡ νῦν Ἑλλὰς καλουμένη οὐ πάλαι βεβαίως οἰκουμένη].[52]

The present participle could better be called a "present-and-imperfect" participle. Its essential difference from the aorist participle is not temporal but aspectual. The last sentence of the decree of Teisamenos can best be rendered:

> Let the laws, as they come to be validated, be inscribed on the wall,

---

51. M. Ostwald, *From Popular Sovereignty to the Sovereignty of Law* (Berkeley: University of California Press, 1986), 519; Robertson (n. 49 above) 46-49; cf. Rhodes, "The Athenian Code of Laws," 98-99.

52. Thuc. 1.2.1. Further examples occur at Thuc. 2.29.1; Lys. 12.64; Xen. *Mem.* 1.2.17-18; *Anab.* 3.2.17; Dem. 19.129; *Isai.* 2.45; Hom. *Od.* 12.439-40 (*krinōn;* Horace understood the reference to the past when he wrote *diiudicata lite* at *Carm.* 3.5.53-56); cf. W.W. Goodwin: *Syntax of the Moods and Tenses of the Greek Verb* (London: Macmillan, 1889), 47-48.

where they were previously inscribed, for anyone who wishes to inspect.

This rendering makes the provisions of the decree cohere better than the proposed alternative does. It is also supported by the ensuing comment of Andokides, quoted above. That is, the laws were to be inscribed on the wall, where laws were previously inscribed, as the decree said. Andokides added that they were inscribed in the stoa. He addressed his speech in 400/399 B.C. to an audience of Athenians, who knew about the work recently completed under the decree of Teisamenos. So it is to be inferred that the laws after ratification were inscribed on a wall in the stoa.

The current challenge to the belief that the laws were revised asserts that Andokides erred in saying that the laws were inscribed in the stoa.[53] The challenge appears to rest on two arguments. First, the decree of Teisamenos provides for keeping the laws of Solon and Drakon in force, and so (it is said) the scope for additional measures would be small. Second, although Andokides (1.85-89) says that there was a general scrutiny of the laws, the decree of Teisamenos does not provide for a general scrutiny, and supposedly the decree is better evidence than the assertions of the orator. The conclusion is drawn that from 403/2 B.C., as from 410/9 B.C., the recorders were merely to transcribe the laws, that is, collect the scattered records with a view to stocking a central archive. Where contradictions were discovered, they were to be resolved by the council and assembly or from 403/2 B.C. for reasons of economy, by the board of lawgivers. Consequently some measures, such as the law of Drakon on homicide, were published anew on stone. But it is concluded, there was no general publication of the whole list of current laws.

The first argument rests on a misunderstanding. The grammatical structure of a decree, such as the decree of Teisamenos, is not a guide to its operative force. If a decree says that all As shall be p except for those As that are q, one cannot tell whether the majority of As will become p or not; that is, one cannot tell whether the purpose of the decree is to make some As p or to protect others from change. The decree of Teisamenos provides for observing the laws of Solon and

---

53. Indeed Robertson ("The Laws of Athens," 62) calls this statement of Andokides "a patent falsehood." It is difficult to see why Robertson considers it false. It is also difficult to believe that Andokides would assert a patent falsehood on a matter so well known at the time to his audience.

Drakon and making additional laws where needed. This grammatical structure does not show whether the bulk of the laws emerging from the procedure would be new ones or measures of the ancient lawgivers.

The other argument rests on an oversight of a different kind. The decree of Teisamenos presupposes that other measures toward revision of the laws had been passed and were being implemented. It mentions two bodies of lawgivers: the "drafters" chosen by the council, and the "ratifiers," who number five hundred and have been chosen by their fellow demesmen. Thus it presupposes measures that ordered the selection of these two bodies of men. Mentioning the oath to be sworn by the ratifiers, the decree presupposes that a measure had been passed or was about to be passed to specify the terms of the oath. In short the decree of Teisamenos was only one of several measures that set the work of legal reform in motion. Toward reconstructing that work, it is reasonable to draw with caution on the explanatory comments of Andokides, because he was talking about things that his audience knew. Moreover, in the course of those comments, he cited five "supplementary" measures, as they may be called, and had them read out by the secretary to the court. It is time to take leave of the challenge and pay attention to the supplementary measures; for they clarify the work of reform that was in progress from 403/2 B.C. to 400/399 B.C.

The five measures are (Andokides 1.85–89):

1. The magistracies [*archai*] shall not observe any unwritten law on any subject.
2. No decree of the council or of the assembly [*dēmos*] shall have greater validity than a law.
3. No law shall be made about a single person, as distinct from the same law for all Athenians, except with the approval of six thousand voting secretly.
4. Judgments of lawsuits and settlements reached by arbitration shall be valid, provided that they came about while the city had *dēmokratia*.
5. The laws made in and after the archonship of Eukleides shall be observed.

As a whole these measures answer the question, what henceforth shall be recognized as valid law. The first and the fifth measures are of importance here. Together they provide that officers shall only uphold measures ratified in written form in or after the year 403/2 B.C., the archonship of Eukleides. The restriction applied not only to administrative activities of public officers but also to trials. In the procedure preliminary to a trial the parties put their documents, including laws, into vessels that were then sealed, and only documents from the vessels could be cited in the trial.[54] The Athenians continued their habit of referring to their laws as laws of Solon, or of Drakon for laws on homicide. Some of the laws attributed by orators to the ancient lawgivers were of later date.[55] It is impossible to tell how many of the laws in the compilation completed in 400/399 were new and how many were measures of Solon (or Drakon) that were now renewed. What matters is that in consequence of the reform carried out in 403/2–400/399, the Athenians had a complete and authoritative list of laws.

The decree of Teisamenos provided that the task of ratifying new measures proposed for laws should be performed by the five hundred lawgivers in collaboration with the council. During the reform or a little later a regular procedure was instituted for amending the laws (*nomoi*). It had two characteristics. First the procedure could only be initiated by a vote of the assembly on the question whether the current laws were satisfactory or needed change. Second the final decision, which chose between the current law and the new proposal, was taken not by the assembly but by a board of lawgivers (*nomothetai*) similar in composition to a court.[56] The pattern of behavior agrees with the tradition that said that Solon had made laws at the bidding of the Athenians (see at n. 43 above). Only the command of the Athenians could initiate the procedure, but the authority ratifying laws was the single lawgiver, in the time of Solon, or a panel, probably in multiples of five hundred, in the fourth century.

There were two judicial procedures for safeguarding the laws. The *graphē paranomōn* upheld the second of the supplementary measures listed above. After a decree had been passed by the assembly, any Athenian not disqualified by *atimia* could prosecute the author of the decree

---

54. Ar. *AP.* 53.2.
55. Andok. 1.95–96; Dem. 20.89–90.
56. The most informative text is Dem. 24.20–38. See also Dem. 20.89–100; Aischin. 3.38–39. For a good account, reference may be made to M.H. Hansen, "*Nomos* and *psephisma* in Fourth-Century Athens," *GRBS* 19 (1978): 315–30. Several laws regulating the procedure are distinguished by Hansen, "Athenian *nomothesia*," *GRBS* 26 (1985): 345–71; the two characteristics noted in the text are constant.

by complaining that it conflicted with the laws. This procedure existed as early as 415 B.C.⁵⁷ Evidently, even before the legal reforms of 410–399, the Athenians believed that laws ought to have greater validity than decrees. The other procedure was the *graphē nomon mē epitēdeion theinai*. After a new law had been ratified by a panel of lawgivers, any Athenian not disqualified could prosecute its author by complaining that the new law was inexpedient. If the new law conflicted with an earlier law and did not repeal it explicitly, the same judicial procedure could be employed. This procedure is first attested for 382/1 B.C., when the author of a measure was convicted and executed.⁵⁸ One may well suppose that the procedure was introduced to protect the "code of 403," as it may be called.

Athens has not yielded any such inscribed list of laws as has been found at Gortyn. The extant measures attributed to Solon have been collected, and several *nomoi* current in the fourth century are known.⁵⁹ Something can be said about the arrangement of the code of 403. For on the eleventh day of each year the assembly was invited to vote on the question, whether amendments were needed, and on this occasion the laws were presented in four categories: laws concerning the council, common laws, laws bearing on the nine archons, and laws concerning the other officers.⁶⁰ Enough Athenian laws are preserved to show that the formulation was often casuistic, as at Gortyn; that is, a law often began with a protasis, "If someone does such and such a thing," or "Whoever does such and such a thing." So one may recall the possibility (mentioned at n. 19 above) that some Athenian laws were written down by the *thesmothetai* even before the time of Solon. The development may have started from judgments in particular cases. Then some general rules may have been formulated from those judgments. Finally Solon wrote an extensive list of rules, incorporating those that had already been reduced to writing. The Athenian concept of law that resulted from this process can be ascertained from the oath sworn by Athenian judges.

---

57. Andok. 1.17 and 22.

58. Dem. 24.138. For fuller discussion of Athenian principles of legislation and for references see Sealey, *Athenian Republic*, 32–52.

59. E. Ruschenbusch, *Solonos Nomoi* (Wiesbaden: Steiner, 1968). A provisional list of *nomoi* for the fourth century has been compiled by M.H. Hansen, "Did the Athenian *ecclesia* Legislate after 403/2 B.C.?" *GRBS* 20 (1979): 27–53, at 39–43; inscriptions discovered since 1979 add to it.

60. Dem. 24.20. The same arrangement can be traced in parts of Ar. *AP.* 43–62.

Oaths, Gaps, and Codes

Judges (*dikastai*) in classical Athens were drawn from a list of six thousand citizens. The list was revised each year. To qualify for inclusion in the list, an Athenian had to be at least thirty years old and he had to swear an oath. The oath has been reconstructed from quotations and allusions in speeches.[61] Its opening clause said:

> I will vote in accordance with the laws and with the decrees of the people of Athens and of the council of five hundred, and on matters where there are no laws, I will vote in accordance with the most just opinion.

The oath divides the duty of the judge into two parts. On the one hand some possible occurrences have been foreseen in the laws (and in the decrees, for by the time whence the full text of the opening clause is attested, the Athenians had achieved a clear distinction between measures of the two kinds). The laws (and the decrees) tell the judge what to do about such occurrences. On the other hand situations arise that have not been foreseen recognizably in the written provisions. The judge is to decide disputes arising in these situations at his discretion, that is, "in accordance with the most just opinion." In an Athenian court each litigant presented his opinion, and the judge had merely to choose between the two. As the oath shows, the Athenians believed that there were laws but there were also gaps between the laws; occurrences not foreseen in the laws fell in the gaps.[62]

As was noted previously, the laws of Gortyn drew the same distinction between the two tasks of a judge. The laws had provided in advance that on some matters the testimony of witnesses or the sworn declaration of a party should be decisive. On these matters the judge had a merely declaratory function; he issued an order in accordance with the testimony or declaration. But on other matters the judge was to swear an oath and make a determination in the light of the contentions; that is, he

---

61. M. Fränkel, "Der attische Heliasteneid," *Hermes* 13 (1878): 452-66.
62. The study by E. Ruschenbusch (*"Dikastērion pantōn kyrion,"* *Historia* 6 [1957]: 257-65, especially 264-65) is fundamental for the theory of gaps. Ostwald (*From Popular Sovereignty,* 5-6) has tried to challenge the findings but he does not consider the oath of *dikastai*.

was to decide the issue at his discretion. The theory of gaps is evident in the Gortynian distinction, just as in the oath of Athenian judges.

The same theory is illustrated in inscribed laws of two other cities. An inscription found at Eresos on Lesbos comes from the time of the successors of Alexander and quotes the oath sworn there by judges. The oath begins with the undertaking:

> I will judge the dispute at law in accordance with the laws, in so far as the points at issue are in the laws, but I will judge all other points diligently in whatever way is best and most just.[63]

Again, an inscription of the sixth century B.C. from Naupaktos or perhaps from Aitolia deals with succession to property. It states the order in which close relatives are to inherit; if none of these is alive, the property is to be divided between the other relatives "in accordance with what is just" (*ka to dikaion*). Here too the distinction is between the written law (*tethmos,* line 1) and the most just opinion for the judge(s) to follow.[64]

The theory of gaps, as it has come to be called, is not a modern hypothesis. It is a principle of adjudication observed in Greek cities. Essentially it distinguishes between the two tasks to be performed by the judge, according as there are or are not laws applicable to the case before him. It is not difficult to account for the prevalence of this principle of adjudication. One has but to suppose that judicial procedures for peaceful settlement of disputes were practised well before laws were issued in writing. That supposition is independently probable; for the *Works and Days* of Hesiod and the *Iliad* tell of judicial settlement of disputes but have no hint of any written laws. When laws were issued in writing, the task was carried out in the light of past experience in settling disputes. So generalized cases were stated in casuistic form with the appropriate judgment. It was understood that other cases, which fell outside or between the generalized provisions, would occur. These were to be decided, as before, by the judges at discretion. Thus conceived, the written laws reduced the scope for judiciary discretion, but the traditional procedures of discretionary judgment remained in force for the limitless expanse of occurrences not foreseen in the laws.

The historical significance of the theory of gaps can best be recognized

---

63. Tod. no. 191, lines 87–92.
64. Meiggs and Lewis no. 13, lines 3–6, explained correctly by M. Gagarin, *Early Greek Law* (Berkeley: University of California Press, 1986), 94–95.

by contrast with Roman practice, as developed by jurisconsults. In Rome the law was first stated in the Twelve Tables. But from an early time Romans learned to argue by analogy from the provisions of that code in order to formulate rules on matters not explicitly covered. A simple illustration, often quoted, will clarify the mode of inference. The Twelve Tables included these three provisions:

1. If a man died leaving no descendants and no will, his nearest agnatic relative should inherit his property (V, 4).
2. If a freedman died leaving no descendants and no will, his former master should inherit his property (V, 8).
3. If a man died leaving a minor son and did not name a guardian by will, his agnatic relatives became guardians of the son (V, 6).

From these rules a fourth was inferred: if a freedman was a minor, his former master and the sons of the former master were his guardians. Gaius the jurist states the fourth rule and says that it was reached *per interpretationem* (1.165). It is easy to see that the fourth rule is implied in some way by the other three. But it is also important to recognize that the fourth rule was not stated explicitly but reached by a process of inference.

Roman jurisconsults employed interpretation extensively to develop the law.[65] The starting point could be other authoritative documents, notably the edict of the urban praetor, in addition to the Twelve Tables. The word *analogy* is sometimes employed to state the nature of legal reasoning in the most general way.[66] More particular ways of applying analogical argument can be recognized. One of them, for example, is definition of words employed in laws. Aristotle (*Rhetoric* 1.1374a1-9) saw the need to define offenses, such as theft, but there is no reason to think that any Greek system of law attempted definition. An Athenian law provided a remedy for "outrage" (*hybris*). The word was not defined but apparently embraced any purported injury to the person. The law served to bring the complaint into court so that the judges could decide by vote whether it was justified and, if so, what penalty the offender should undergo.[67] In Athenian courts, parties might engage in legal

---

65. H.J. Wolff, *Roman Law: An Historical Introduction* (Norman: University of Oklahoma Press), 63-65.

66. H.S. Maine, *Ancient Law* (1861; reprint, London: Dent, 1965), 11, 23.

67. Dem. 21.47; Ruschenbusch, "*Hybreōs graphē,*" ZSR 82 (1965): 302-9. For a different

reasoning in an attempt to extend the law by analogy, to inquire into the intention of the lawgiver, or to bring inferences from acknowledged laws to bear on a novel case.[68] But neither the Athenians nor any other Greek city is known to have endorsed the further belief that an authoritative ruling could be reached by legal reasoning.

It was left to the Romans, in particular Roman jurists, to take that further step. Modern systems have inherited the same belief, although the machinery for delivering an authoritative ruling is different. In Rome the ruling was the opinion of a jurisconsult, who served as a legal adviser. In modern systems, the ruling on a question of law is made by a judge. This is the function of the judge both in systems of the Common Law, where the ruling constitutes precedent, and in those of the Civil Law. The difference is that in the Common Law the ruling of a judge is law, but in the Civil Law it is an application of law. In both systems and in Rome authoritative exposition and eventually extension of the law require a learned jurist, someone who is superior in his understanding of the law to the average man. Roman and modern systems require professional lawyers, even though the profession had a markedly different structure in Rome than in modern countries.

The distinctive character of the Greek concept of law can be seen in a different and perhaps more informative light. Let it be supposed that two persons have a dispute and consider bringing it to court. Often the most satisfactory outcome would be a settlement reached by the parties themselves out of court. To encourage this result, Athens in the fourth century B.C. insisted that every private dispute should go first to an arbitrator. He had no authority to impose a solution, but he tried to mediate a settlement, and the case only went on to court if his efforts failed.[69] In modern systems attorneys often try to negotiate a settlement out of court. But suppose that no such settlement is reached and the case comes to court. Then the law is approached as a source of help toward discovering a settlement that both parties can accept; the judge's task is to expound the law for this purpose, and court proceedings can be interrupted if either or both parties, on gaining a better knowledge of the law, become willing in consequence to settle out of court. For the law (that is, the

---

view, attempting a definition of *hybris* as distinct from *aikeia*, see D.M. MacDowell, "*Hybris* in Athens," *Greece and Rome*, 2d ser., 23 (1976): 14–31.

68. M. Hillgruber: *Die zehnte Rede des Lysias* (= Untersuchungen zur antiken Literatur und Geschichte, Band 29, Berlin and New York: de Gruyter, 1988) 105–20.

69. Ar. *AP.* 53; cf. chap. 6 of this book.

body of law, *ius*) is believed to be a continuum, embracing all relations between persons. Particular rules (*leges*) are merely salient parts of it. The law in Rome and in modern systems has no gaps.

It follows that the word *code,* if understood in its modern implications, is not applicable to Greek lists of laws.[70] For in modern systems the law is conceived as being present in all dealings between persons, and so it offers its help toward solving any dispute that may arise. The *leges,* the rules stated in the code, are merely salient manifestations of the body of law, *ius,* from which they spring. A Greek "code" was no more than a list of *leges;* it left indeterminate a residual area in the gaps, and any dispute arising in that area was to be decided by judges at discretion.

To recognize the distinctive character of Greek, or particularly Athenian, law does not amount to saying that the Roman and modern concept of law as a continuum is better. The Athenian system, the Greek system of which the functioning can be reconstructed in some degree, was different but not necessarily inferior. One can recognize merits and defects in different systems. The preceding paragraphs may have alerted the gentle reader to merits in the Roman and modern systems. Perhaps a defect has also come to light. If law is a continuum, it is recondite beyond everyday comprehension. So there must be professional experts to expound it, and professions sometimes try to increase their power. But historical inquiry need not embark on the limitless enterprise of assessing merits and defects. Its task is to understand. It must recognize that the Greeks had no legal profession and did not conceive of law as a continuum. To put the matter in positive terms, they had amateur administration of justice and they had the theory of gaps, and these two things were causally interrelated.

Yet the development might have been different. A solitary text tells of an authoritative ruling issued in a Greek city on a basis of legal reasoning. The text is a story told by Polybios (12.16) about a dispute that arose in the city of Lokroi in Italy. The point of the story concerned temporary possession of a disputed thing while the case was *sub iudice.* Apart from the eventual question of ownership, to be decided in a definitive trial, the issue might arise, who should have the thing provisionally until the court met and rendered its judgment. A law attributed to Zaleukos and current at Lokroi said that "until the court gave judgment, provisional

---

70. Cf. J.W. Jones, *The Law and Legal Theory of the Greeks* (Oxford: Oxford University Press, 1956), 102 n. 4; Stroud, *Drakon's Law,* 9 n. 18.

possession of the things in dispute should be assigned to the party from whom they had been taken away."

Two men, who may be called A and B, disagreed over a slave, and A was in possession of the slave. But when A went away on a journey, B went to the field where the slave was, took him away by force and put him in B's house. When A came back two days later, he took the slave from B's house and went with the slave to the magistracy (*archē*). A said that he ought to have provisional possession, since the slave had been taken from him. But B said that he ought to have provisional possession, since the slave had been taken from his house. The magistrates were at a loss and consulted the *kosmopolis*. The latter ruled in favor of A. For, he said, "taking away" (*agōgē*) in the law meant taking from someone who had been in undisputed possession for a period of time. But B denied that that interpretation was the intention of the lawgiver. So the *kosmopolis* challenged B to take their difference of interpretation to the body called the Thousand. That is, B and the *kosmopolis* would each present his own interpretation at a session of the Thousand, and nooses would be made ready for hanging the one whose opinion the Thousand rejected. B declined the challenge and said that the risks were not equal, for he himself was young but the *kosmopolis* was nearly ninety years of age and had only a few years to live. So the magistrates followed the opinion of the *kosmopolis*.

Nothing more is known about a Lokrian officer bearing the title of *kosmopolis*. The story may have gained in the telling; other stories were told about codes of law that could only be amended on the proposal of a man who stood with a noose around his neck in front of the legislative assembly (see at n. 4 above). Even if the story is wholly fictitious, it shows that some Greeks thought about the possibility of an authoritative ruling on a question of law. Moreover, the law about provisional possession may be genuine, since its probable purpose can be detected. This law says nothing about ownership; in assigning provisional possession it does not even create a presumption about ownership. It must be regarded from the standpoint of a man from whom something has been taken. He believes that the thing is rightfully his. By assigning provisional possession to him, the Lokrian law encourages him to go to law instead of having recourse to self-help. Thus this law pursues the same purpose as the first section of the code of Gortyn. In the story told by Polybios, A endangered his right of provisional possession by having recourse to self-help. Possibly the story was invented or elaborated to point this moral.

Conceivably proof of ownership had become so difficult and costly at Lokroi that litigants were content to desist from their dispute, once provisional possession had been assigned. But this speculation does not lead further. The most suggestive parts of the story are the role and the ruling of the *kosmopolis*. His ruling has invited further thought. Some authorities explain it by paying attention to the lengthy period during which A had had possession of the slave. For, it is suggested, one's economic plans are disturbed if one loses something after a protracted period of possession, but they are not disturbed if one loses possession after only two days.[71] An alternative explanation would draw attention to the undisputed character of A's possession. That is, the ruling of the *kosmopolis* restored a condition in which B had previously acquiesced.

It is surprising that in the story the person giving the ruling is specified by the title of an office, not by a name. He does not exercise official authority in the story. Instead he states a reason for assigning provisional possession to A. His role is that of a man respected for his superior understanding of law. He behaves after the manner of a Roman jurisconsult. He intervenes only when the magistrates approach him; they detach a question of law from the total dispute and refer it to him. His opinion carries weight, not in virtue of the authority of his office, but because B shrinks from the risk of challenging it. In effect the *kosmopolis* interprets and applies the law and in doing so he expands it. Since he gives a reason for his ruling, he is in an intellectually different situation from the Athenian *dikastai*, who swore to vote "in accordance with the laws . . . and on matters where there are no laws, in accordance with the most just opinion." If the story were first attested a hundred years later, one might suspect that the practice of Roman jurisconsults had influenced Lokroi.

The Lokrian story is an isolated phenomenon. It suggests that the Greek intellect might have taken the path followed by the jurists of Rome. Aristotle's demand for definition of legal terms points in the same direction. Yet as has been seen, Greek practice, attested at Athens, Gortyn, Eresos, and Naupaktos or Aitolia, did not follow that path. Greeks had no collective word, equivalent to *ius,* for a body of law,

---

71. A. Kränzlein, *Eigentum und Besitz im griechischen Recht des fünften und vierten Jahrhunderts v. Chr.* (Berlin: Duncker, 1963), 155-58.

since they did not recognize law as a seamless web. Instead they thought that particular laws foresaw some eventualities but the residual area of human behavior fell in the gaps between the laws and was to be regulated, when necessary, at the discretion of *dikastai*.

It is easy to see that this concept of laws as discrete things could arise from the historical process of issuing laws in writing, especially if that process had come about piecemeal, in response to judgments made in single disputes, as suggested above. The issuing of laws (and eventually of compilations of laws) in writing was an experience common to many Greek states and it brought into being a common concept of law. So the next chapter will study the question of the unity of Greek law. The present chapter has maintained that compilations of prescriptive law were a Greek innovation, not known in the early civilizations of the Near East, even though the Hittites may have come close to it. The chapter has also recognized the probability that the Greeks learned to issue single laws, and eventually compilations of laws, in written form because they already had a procedure for judicial settlement of disputes; laws developed from judgments when judgments were generalized. So chapters 4 and 5 will return to procedure.

CHAPTER 3

The Unity of Greek Law

The Limits to Inquiry into Substantive Law

It was maintained in chapter 1 that the historian of Greek law should not be content to ascertain rules. He should also search for underlying ideas that are realized in the rules, and the trio of principles, concepts, and aims was propounded as a path that should lead to discovering such ideas. But in chapter 2 it became apparent that Greeks regarded the laws listed in their codes as discrete rules; they did not recognize an underlying body of thought expressed in the particular provisions. Sometimes men of speculative bent tried to look beyond the bare utterances of the statutes; Aristotle, for example, recognized the need to define offenses, and pleaders could argue from analogy. Even so, for the most part the quest for principles, concepts, and aims is an inquiry that seeks to probe beneath the surface of Greek legal utterances. On the other hand in chapter 2 it also became apparent that the work of issuing written lists of laws was an experience common to many Greek cities, and it had a common consequence in an underlying concept of law.

Postponing consideration of procedure, the present chapter will try to probe beneath the surface of substantive law. So it must acknowledge a major obstacle in the scanty and sporadic nature of the evidence. A particular illustration may exemplify this point. In the hilly lands bordering the Mediterranean it can happen that two men own different parcels of land on the same slope and water flowing from the field of one man to that of the other causes damage. In the agrarian conditions of antiquity this predicament could lead to disputes. That it did so is known from a lengthy title in the Digest, *de aqua et (actione) aquae pluviae arcendae*. The remedial action was mentioned in the Twelve

Tables. It was unusual among Roman actions in that a defendant who lost his case was only required to stop the damage for the future, not to pay compensation for damage already done. Many questions arose: Should the remedy be provided solely if the water was wholly rain or even if it was other water increased by rain? Should it be provided only if the flow of the water had been affected by human action? Does a plaintiff have a remedy if the flow of water damages a mound on his neighbor's land and thereby causes loss to the plaintiff? Roman jurists gave opinions on these and other questions about this action; they built up a large body of law on the subject.[1] The same predicament arose in Greece but is known only from a single speech of Demosthenes (55). Nothing is known about treatment of the subject in other cities. The speech itself is of some importance for the law of actions but tells the reader little about substantive law.

A more general view of the difficulty can be reached by reviewing law in its traditional branches. Teaching in the second century A.D., Gaius divided Roman law into three parts and subdivided some of these. There is no way to discover whether he invented or inherited this classification. It has been kept in subsequent expositions of Roman law. Indeed some of its features can still be recognized in accounts of modern systems of the Civil Law, even though these have developed their own shape. Its tested convenience recommends it in the approach to Greek law.

Gaius divided law into the law of persons, the law of things, and the law of actions. The second of these underwent subdivision. Things usually become of interest to the law when someone asserts rights to them. The law of things is subdivided into property and obligations. For one's assets, the things with which one is intimately concerned, are of two kinds. There are, first, the things that one has (property), and, second, the things owed to one (obligations). A physician, for example, may have a house, some medical equipment, and some money; his recent patients may owe him fees for services, and it may be customary to pay these at the beginning of the ensuing month. If he dies in the middle of the month, his executor will have to pay attention both to the property and to the fees due; these two things constitute the assets of the deceased. The law of property is mainly concerned with ways of acquiring property. Acquisition is of two kinds. On the one hand one may acquire particular

---

1. *Digest* 39.3; for discussion see A. Watson, *The Law of Property in the Later Roman Republic* (Oxford: Oxford University Press, 1968), 155–75.

things, and so the law provides conveyances or ways of transferring ownership from one person to another. On the other hand one may acquire the totality of a person's assets if one is his heir when he dies (universal succession). Obligations were recognized by Gaius as of two kinds: those arising from contract and those arising from delict.

The law of actions, the ways of settling disputes, will be postponed to the next two chapters, and delict will be treated under the law of actions. Adopting the classification of Gaius, one might look in Greek law for these themes:

1. Law of persons.
    a) Something can be said about the statuses of citizen, alien, and slave.
    b) Rather more is known about marriage and kinship.
2. Acquisition of particular things.
    There is a modicum of information about purchase and sale of houses in Athens in the fourth century. It will be noted shortly.
3. Acquisition by universal succession.
    On this there is relatively full information from Athens and from Gortyn.
4. Contract.
    There is little information about the legal aspects of contractual obligations and it will be noted shortly.

From this list it appears that the field of Greek substantive law most promising for comparative inquiry is that of kinship, marriage, and inheritance (1*b*, 3). Something will be said first about house purchase (2) and contract (4), and rather more will be said about status (1*a*). Then the field of kinship, marriage, and inheritance will be studied in relation to the question of the unity of Greek law, for that question has lately provoked discussion. Subheadings to be recognized within this field will be inheritance, women, and the female orphan, a type of woman who attracted much legal thought among Greeks.

As observed, there is a modicum of information about the rules governing purchase and sale of houses in Athens in the fourth century. The purchaser had to pay a tax equal to a hundredth of the price. When the parties had reached agreement on the transaction and on the price, an interval of (probably) six days passed before the house ceased to belong to the seller and began to belong to the buyer. Probably the interval was intended to protect the seller from parting with his property in an ill-considered way.² Otherwise not much is known about the legal aspects of acquiring particular things or of contractual obligations. Some informative speeches about loans for maritime ventures are preserved, but they reveal more to the economic historian than to the comparative jurist.³ It may well be that any agreement seriously intended was an enforceable contract, with witnesses often invited and writing employed as safeguards against misunderstanding and default.

This possibility suggests a further speculation. To the Romanist Greek law is remarkable for its relative lack of forms. Although utterances in specific words were required for the Athenian contract of betrothal,⁴ most transactions appear to have owed their validity merely to the intention of the parties; written records may often have been made and witnessed, but these were conveniences, not elements of the transaction. There is no trace of any required set of words or gestures comparable to the Roman *stipulatio* or *mancipatio per aes et libram*.⁵ The rigidity of Roman forms stimulated praetors to develop more flexible procedures in addition. The *stipulatio*, for example, was in many circumstances inconvenient, and so the praetors brought into being other types of contract, though not a general theory of contract.⁶ Similarly, the conveyance called *mancipatio per aes et libram* could not be employed if one of the parties to a transaction was not a Roman citizen, or if the thing to be transferred did not belong within the limited list of *res mancipi*. The praetors met the deficiency by recognizing and regulating acquisition by prescription.⁷ Likewise, Roman law learned at an early stage to recognize and protect possession in some circumstances without

---

2. W. Schwahn, "Der Hauskauf in Athen," *Hermes* 69 (1934): 119-20.

3. Dem. 32, [Dem.] 33, 34, 35, 56; cf. G.M. Calhoun, "Risk in Sea Loans in Ancient Athens," *Journal of Economic and Business History* 2 (1929-30): 561-84.

4. Hdt. 6.130; Menand. *Dys.* 842-43. Parts of the form of words are also cited at Menand. *Mis.* 444-45; *Perikeir.* 1013-14; *Sam.* 726-27.

5. Gaius (3.92-93) says that the stipulation is peculiar to Roman law. The form of *mancipatio* can be recovered from Gaius 2.104 with 1.132 and 2.22-23. Rome had other procedural forms, but some of these passed out of use without being incorporated into praetorian law; such was the *deductio moribus* of Cic. *Caec.* 20, 27; see B.W. Frier, *The Rise of the Roman Jurists: Studies in Cicero's "pro Caecina"* (Princeton: Princeton University Press, 1985), 78-92.

6. A. Watson, *The Evolution of Law* (Baltimore: Johns Hopkins University Press, 1985), 4-28.

7. B. Nicholas, *An Introduction to Roman Law* (Oxford: Oxford University Press, 1962), 105-6, 120-28.

inquiring into ownership.⁸ Greeks did not attain this insight, as far as is known;⁹ the law about provisional possession at Lokroi, noted at the end of chapter 2, is not extensive enough in scope to constitute an exception. In disputes about property Greek courts tried to discover which of the two parties was the owner.¹⁰ Likewise no Greek system of law is known to have recognized prescriptive acquisition. The Athenians recognized a limitation of five years on actions for property, but limitation is not prescription.¹¹ Accordingly, just as the rigidity of pristine forms challenged Roman praetors to develop the law of property and the law of contracts extensively, so it may be suggested, Greek legal thought failed to go far in these fields because it was not constrained by any such rigidity.

Status

The legal condition of the citizen, the alien, and the slave in Greek cities merits attention because this part of the law of persons offers some prospect of significant conclusions. Slavery varies markedly in character in different systems of law and even within the same system at different times. The term *unfree* is to be preferred, for it does not pretend to precision. The law-code of Gortyn mentions unfree persons of varying kinds. There is the *woikeus*, or agrarian serf. People of this condition live in the countryside and have farm animals; their marriages are recognized. There are also references in the laws to the domestic female slave and to the slave bought from the marketplace.¹² In classical Athens the law distinguished between free persons and slaves, and although the

---

8. Nicholas, *Introduction to Roman Law,* 107-15.
9. See H.J. Wolff, *ZSR* 81 (1964): 333-40 (review of Kränzlein); cf. A.R.W. Harrison, *The Law of Athens,* vol. 1, *The Family and Property* (Oxford: Oxford University Press, 1968), 200-205.
10. The limitation of five years is mentioned by Dem. 36.25-27; 38.17-18. One cannot be sure how extensive it was. On the difference between prescription and limitation see Nicholas, *Introduction to Roman Law,* 120-21.
11. M. Kaser ("Der altgriechische Eigentumsschutz," *ZSR* 64 [1944]: 134-205, at 184) maintained that the issue in *diadikasia* was "das bessere, das stärkere Recht zum Besitz." That is ultimately true of every suit for property in any system of law. The court decides, in the light of currently available information, which party has the better right to possess the thing. It is possible that some time after judgment has been given, new evidence will be discovered and provide grounds for opening the case anew.
12. The *woikeus: IC* 4. 72: IV, 31-43. His marriage: ibid. II, 27-28; III, 40-44; III, 52 to IV, 8; IV, 18-21. The domestic female slave: ibid. II, 11-16. The slave bought from the marketplace: ibid. VII, 10-15.

latter differed much in economic condition, their legal status was uniform. Conditions before the work of Solon are more elusive. The character of his measure of liberation, the *seisachtheia,* is disputed. An attractive hypothesis says that the condition of the people liberated was not a recent consequence of loans and debt but a traditional status of personal dependence and land tenure.[13] Elsewhere on the mainland of European Greece, there were unfree persons who worked the land: the helots of Sparta, the *penestai* of Thessaly, the *gymnētes* of Argos.[14] Little is known about them. The process of migration and settlement in Greece may have produced unfree status in great variety. Like many nations of antiquity, the Greeks recognized that much necessary work is disagreeable and believed that it requires workers who lack freedom.

Among free inhabitants classical Athens distinguished between citizens and metics (resident aliens). Athenian citizenship was not a condition fixed once and for all when a half-legendary *synoikismos* produced the city. On the contrary, the emergence and development of public institutions was a protracted process, and with the institutions citizenship came into being and grew in its content of rights and obligations.[15] By 451/0 B.C., citizenship had become so weighty and distinctive that a law was passed restricting it to persons whose parents were both citizens (chap. 2, at n. 46). The word "metic" (*metoikos*) first occurs in the plays of Aischylos.[16] Metic status may well have arisen at the time when citizenship was crystallizing; the two conditions may have developed in counterpoint. It will be fruitful to pause briefly over the resident alien.

In classical Athens one could attain metic status in each of two ways. On the one hand, there were free persons who migrated to Athens and

---

13. A. Andrewes, *Cambridge Ancient History,* 2d ed., 3.2 (Cambridge: Cambridge University Press, 1982), 377-82.

14. Pollux 3.83.

15. This is the central discovery of P.B. Manville, *The Origin of Citizenship in Ancient Athens* (Princeton: Princeton University Press, 1990). See also J.K. Davies, "Athenian Citizenship: The Descent Group and the Alternatives," *CJ* 73 (1977-78): 105-21; R. Sealey, "How Citizenship and the City Began in Athens," *AJAH* 8 (1983): 97-129.

16. Aisch. *Pers.* 319; *Seven* 548; *Agam.* 57; *Cho.* 971. Other derivatives of the same root occur at *Supp.* 609 and *Eum.* 1018. The word occurs in an inscription of the deme Skambonidai ca. 460: *IG* 1³. 244C, l. 8. *Metaoikos* occurs in an earlier inscription, perhaps of the late sixth century; see K. Baba, "On Kerameikos Inv. I 388 (*SEG* 12. 79). A Note on the Formation of the Athenian Metic-Status," *ABSA* 79 (1984): 1-5. D. Whitehead, *The Ideology of the Athenian Metic* (Cambridge: Cambridge University Press, 1977), 140-47, argues that the legal status of metic came into being about the time of the reforms of Kleisthenes.

settled there. Metics had to pay a tax, the *metoikion*, at the annual rate of twelve drachmas for a man and six drachmas for a woman.[17] Like citizens, they could be conscripted for military service.[18] In view of these burdens metics had to be distinguished from other aliens. It is not unlikely that in the fourth century B.C. an alien in Athens became a metic, liable for the burdens, by staying in Attica a specified number of days, perhaps a month.[19] Historians have often assumed that the free migrant was the typical metic, but metics arose also from a second source. If an Athenian owner manumitted a slave, the former slave became a metic, not a citizen.[20] Being an alien, a metic could not own "land or house" in the Athenian phrase (see below). He required a *prostatēs*, or patron, and it is likely that his living accommodation was a dwelling supplied to him by his *prostatēs* in return for services. So in the time of Aristotle the *prostatēs* had a remedy in the polemarch's court against the metic who did not perform the agreed services; there was a *dikē apostasiou,* if the metic was a former slave, and otherwise a *dikē aprostasiou.*[21]

Apart from this difference in the wording of the actions no difference in status between metics of the two kinds can be discovered. So a question of relative priority arises. Manumission is well attested in Athens during and after the age of the orators and in many other Greek cities, but it is absent from the Homeric poems; Odysseus promises his loyal herdsmen wives, possessions, houses, and other good things, but says nothing about personal freedom.[22] Metic status was probably not known in the Athens of Solon. For a law, attributed to him with high probability, offered

---

17. Harpok. s.v. *metoikion;* Pollux 3.55.
18. Thuc. 2.13.7; cf. *IG* I². 1084.
19. This has been argued by Whitehead, *Ideology,* 7-10. The alternative view, that metic status was a consequence of an intention of permanent residence, has been defended by E. Lévy, "Métèques et droit de résidence" (*L' étranger dans le monde grec.* Actes du colloque organisé par l' Institut d' Etudes Anciennes, Nancy, mai 1987, sous la direction de Louis Raoul. *Travaux et Mémoires de l' Université de Nancy* II. Etudes anciennes 4, 1988): 47-67. But Whitehead's inference from the inscription about Sidonian merchants in Athens (*IG* II². 141 = Tod no. 139, lines 30-36) seems decisive.
20. Harpok. s.v. *metoikion;* cf. Hesych. s.v. *isotelēs;* Whitehead, *Ideology,* 16-17.
21. Ar. *AP.* 58.3; Harpok. s.vv. *apostasiou, aprostasiou;* Poll. 8.35; *Lex. Rhet. Cantab.* 201. The connections have been made by G. Thür, "Wo wohnen die Metöken?" in *Demokratie und Architektur,* ed. W. Schuller, W. Hoepfner, and E.L. Schwandner (Munich: Deutscher Kunstverlag, 1989), 117-21. The fortunes of Alke can be noted as an illustration. She was bought as a slave by Euktemon. His extensive possessions included a *synoikia* (lodging house) in the Kerameikos. After a time Euktemon manumitted Alke and put her in charge of the lodging house (Isai. 6.19-21).
22. *Od.* 21.214-216; cf. 14.64; T. Thalheim, "Freigelassene," *RE* 7:95-100.

citizenship to aliens who settled with their households in Athens to practise a trade.[23] In the classical period such people would have become metics. As remarked earlier (n. 16 above), metic status probably first came to be recognized during or soon after the reforms of Kleisthenes. There are then two possibilities:

1. A regular practice of manumission first came into being some time after metic status had been accorded to free persons who settled in Attica, and the liberated slave was assimilated to the alien of free birth.
2. Manumission is the origin of metic status. The liberated slave was assigned to a free but inferior condition; he was said to "live with" (*metoikein*) the Athenians. During or after the reforms of Kleisthenes, aliens of free birth who settled in Attica were assigned to this condition, although in Solonian law at least some of them had been treated on an equality with native Athenians.

Perhaps the second alternative accounts rather better for the many Athenian utterances that speak contemptuously of metics; they were tolerated and were expected to behave well in return.[24] In any case there was no doubt about the inferiority of their status. They could not own immovable property. This disability is inferred from plentiful inscribed decrees, which grant "capacity to own land and house" (*enktēsis gēs kai oikias*) as a privilege to individual metics. Inscriptions of this content have been found not only in Athens but also in many other Greek cities, from the Peloponnese to Boiotia, Phokis, Thessaly, Eretria, Keos, Delos, Kyme, Phokaia, and other towns.[25] Generally in Greek cities ownership of immovable property was reserved to citizens. At this level there was a common element in the concept of citizenship in the different cities. Its significance can be recognized by contrast with Rome. There, although a free alien could not take part in the conveyance called *mancipatio per aes et libram,* he could acquire property of any kind from a citizen, and a citizen could acquire property of any kind from him. Again, if a Roman owner manumitted a slave, the former slave became a citizen,

---

23. Solon F 75 = Plut. *Sol.* 24.4. On the attribution to Solon, see Davies and Sealey (n. 15 above).
24. Whitehead, *Ideology,* 27–60.
25. T. Thalheim, *"Enktesis," RE* 5:2584–85.

although he still owed some duties to his patron.²⁶ Greeks regarded the citizenship of their cities as a more elevated status. The high regard accorded to the citizen in Greek cities will require further attention at the end of this chapter and in chapter 6. It is a clue to the underlying impulse that made Greeks develop the concept of law, justice, or right.

The Question of Unity

The distinctive way in which Greeks regarded law (the theory of gaps, chap. 2) and the distinctive way in which they regarded citizenship reveal underlying ideas shared by many Greek cities. Approaching the subjects of kinship, marriage, and inheritance, one must confront the question of the unity of Greek law. It is beyond denial that each city, being independent, had its own courts and made its own statutes. But a search for underlying principles must ask whether there were common elements. The merit for raising the question belongs to the late Sir Moses Finley.[27] Reacting against predecessors who had spoken, perhaps too casually, of common juristic outlooks, he expressed a clear view, basing it mainly and rightly on comparison between Athens and Gortyn. The kernel of his argument concerns rules about marriage, legitimacy, the rights of women, and inheritance; it deserves to be quoted:

1. Periclean Athens went as far as it was possible to go in one line of development: restriction of legitimate marriage to members of the citizen body on both sides; the formal requirement of *ekdosis* and *engyesis;* the classification of all children not the offspring of such marriages as "bastards" (*nothoi*), with their consequent exclusion from intestate succession when there were legitimate children, and, at least in the case of children of a "mixed" marriage, from citizenship; denial to women of all rights to an inheritance, of the right to administer or control property, of freedom from tutelage.
2. In the Gortyn code there is no trace of *engyesis* (though that does not necessarily mean that there were "free" marriages); daughters had

---

26. Nicholas, *Introduction to Roman Law,* 72–76, cf. 65. But slaves manumitted informally became Junian Latins, an intermediate status.

27. M.I. Finley, "The Problem of the Unity of Greek Law," in *The Use and Abuse of History* (London: Chatto and Windus, 1975), 134–52. The passage quoted is from p. 139.

mandatory claims to a share in the succession; women owned and controlled property, and an orphaned daughter without brothers had certain freedoms and privileges denied her Athenian counterpart, the *epikleros*.

Some inaccuracies call for immediate note.

1. The Periclean law of 451/0 B.C. restricted citizenship to children whose parents were both citizens. Legitimate marriage was not restricted to members of the citizen body. A male metic could marry a female metic, and disputes on matters of law of the family among metics were received by the polemarch.[28]
2. Many marriages were contracted by *engyēsis* (betrothal) and *ekdosis* (transfer of the bride to the dwelling of the bridegroom). But an *epiklēros* was assigned in marriage to her nearest male relative. That is, the archon adjudicated the woman to the male relative. If more than one relative claimed her, he first called a court into session to decide between the claims. The archon's act of adjudication was called *epidikasia*. Marriages brought about by *epidikasia* and marriages brought about by *engyēsis* and *ekdosis* had equal validity.[29]
3. The children of a marriage brought about by *epidikasia* inherited the property of their maternal grandfather.[30] So it is not true to say that all children not born of an engyetic marriage were classified as bastards or excluded from intestate succession.
4. Athenian women could inherit property. By intestate succession, if

---

28. Ar. *AP.* 58.2–3.
29. Isai. 6.14.
30. See chap. 1 on the *epiklēros*. It is a further question, what happened to the children of two citizens who were united neither by *epidikasia* nor by *engyēsis* and *ekdosis*. The only known case is that of Pamphilos, the son of Mantias and Plangon. Pamphilos received his share of the paternal inheritance: Dem. 39.6; [Dem.] 40.2, 48. The case has recently had careful but inconclusive discussion by C. Carey and R.A. Reid (*Demosthenes: Selected Private Speeches* [Cambridge: Cambridge University Press, 1985], 164–66). All difficulties disappear if one recognizes a difference in the concept of marriage. Modern marriage can only be contracted with the cooperation of a public officer and with registration; dissolution is an act of a court. Athenian marriage was a private arrangement and could be dissolved if the husband merely sent his wife away (*apopempsis*). So the law of succession inquired into the identity and status of the parents but not into the character of their union; see R. Sealey, *Women and Law in Classical Greece* (Chapel Hill: University of North Carolina Press, 1990), 32.

there were no direct descendants of the deceased, his property passed first to his brothers, begotten by the same father, and to children of those brothers. If there were no such persons, it passed to sisters of the deceased, begotten by the same father, and to the children of those sisters. In the further order of succession by kinship, males and persons related through males had precedence, but females were not excluded.[31] Again, the dispute over the inheritance of Pyrrhos arose from the rival claims of two women. One of them, Phile, said that she was the daughter of Pyrrhos. The other denied this and insisted that she herself should inherit as the sister of Pyrrhos.[32] Women could likewise inherit under a will. For example, Dikaiogenes had no children and was killed in a naval battle. His will assigned a third of his estate to his male cousin and the other two thirds in equal shares to his four sisters.[33] In litigation a woman was represented by her male *kyrios* or guardian; he might be her husband or a relative by blood. But forensic speeches regularly specify the women themselves as taking action at law. In court, the relation between a woman and her *kyrios* was that of a modern litigant to his attorney.

5. The laws of Gortyn admittedly do not mention *engyēsis*. Indeed, although they have lengthy rules (VII, 15 to IX, 24) about marrying the heiress or female orphan, they do not say how other women are to be married. Presumably the procedure was too well known to need specification in these laws. So the absence of the word *engyēsis* is not significant. Moreover, the rules include provisions to be followed "if a woman who has been given by her father or brother becomes an heiress" (VIII, 20-22). It follows that a father or brother could give his daughter or sister in marriage. That is *engyēsis*, whatever the word for it may have been in Cretan dialect.

Thus the reasons given by Finley for denying any degree of unity in Greek law are grounded in errors. In studying the field of kinship, marriage, and inheritance, one must be prepared to recognize ideas common to different cities. In approaching this field one should look beyond the rules on the surface of the law (for reasons given in chap. 1). Two systems of law may happen to furnish rules that coincide,

---

31. Isai. 11.1-3; see below at n. 48.
32. Isai. 3.1-3.
33. Isai. 5.5-6.

although they have started from different aims and assumptions. Thus the marriage of a widow to her brother-in-law (levirate marriage, to be noted below) occurred both in Hebrew law and in the Middle Assyrian Laws, but the purpose of the institution was different. In Hebrew law levirate marriage sought to perpetuate the name and inheritance of the deceased, but the Assyrian Laws tried to protect a right that had been acquired through payment of matrimonial gifts (bride-price).[34]

One must look for ideas that underlie the laws. Material is to be drawn mostly from Athens and Gortyn, occasionally from other cities. Furthermore, with a view to determining whether similarities between Greek cities are significant, comparisons should be made with Roman law. For the Romans lived at first in geographic and economic conditions much like those of the Greeks, and so they provide a control group, to borrow a fashionable word.

Inheritance

It was recognized in chapter 1 that the concept of a universal succession, which dominates the Roman law of inheritance, is reflected in Athenian precautions to ensure that the *oikos* should not become empty. The law-code of Gortyn (V, 9–28) states the order of succession to property among relatives. It also orders (XI, 31–42) that, if a man dies owing debts, the heirs may take the property provided that they also pay the debts; if they are not willing to undertake the debts, they surrender the property to the creditors but incur no further liability. A universal succession is evidently assumed.

If the law of inheritance makes a universal succession its point of departure, the difference between inheritance by bequest and inheritance *ab intestato* does not have radical significance. In Rome the duties of the heir, including the tasks of an executor, and the benefits he derived from the inheritance, were in principle the same, whether he was named in a will or succeeded in consequence of kinship (although a will might limit his benefits by creating legacies and *fideicommissa* or trusts). In Athens, as noted in chapter 1, bequest and adoption were scarcely distinguishable. An extant law authorized the practice and imposed restrictions; in particular, if a man had begotten sons who were alive he could

---

34. P. Cruveilhier, "Le lévirat chez les Hébreux et chez les Assyriens," *Revue Biblique* 34 (1925): 524–46.

not adopt.[35] That is, succession by testament was modeled on succession by begotten sons. Adoption was a fiction that treated the adopted person as if he had been born into the family.

The law-code of Gortyn provides for succession by kinsmen in the following order:

1. The inheritance is to pass first to children of the deceased, then to grandchildren, then to great-grandchildren.
2. If there are none of the above, it shall pass to brothers of the deceased, then to their children and grandchildren.
3. If there are none of the above, it shall pass to sisters of the deceased, then their children and grandchildren.[36]

So far the Gortynian laws say nothing about bequest. An argument from silence might or might not be permissible. A later part of the code has rules about adoption, and these are more revealing (X, 33 to XI, 23). An adult man may adopt a son, but a woman or a minor cannot. Adoption is to be carried out "from the stone where proclamations are made in the place of assembly when the citizens have gathered." If there are no children by birth to the adopter, the adoptive son will acquire all the rights and obligations of the adopter; if he is not willing to perform the obligations, the inheritance will pass to the kinsmen of the deceased. But if the adopter has begotten male children or children of both sexes, the adoptive son is to receive a daughter's share (half of a son's share, IV, 37-43) in the inheritance. Likewise, if all the begotten children are female, the adoptive son is to receive a share equal to that of each of them. The adopter may annul the adoption. Again, he must do this "from the stone where proclamations are made in the place of assembly when the citizens have gathered." He is to deposit ten staters with a public officer, who will hand the sum to the man disclaimed.

These rules provide not only for the man who looks ahead to a childless death (childless because he has not begotten children or because his children have died). It could also happen that a man wished to provide against his death while his children were still many years under the age of majority. Such a man might wish to adopt a son, and later, when his children approached maturity, he might wish to annul the adoption. On

---

35. The law is quoted at [Dem.] 46.13; see n. 24 chap. 1, for further references.
36. *IC* IV, 72: V, 9-22. The code adds two further categories (ll. 22-28), but interpretation is uncertain.

the whole the Gortynian rules on adoption give an impression of rigidity in comparison with the flexibility that the Athenian will attained in the age of the orators. The two systems share the basic fiction: the adoptive heir is treated as if he were a son by birth.

In Rome adoption in one form (*adrogatio,* where the person to be adopted was *sui iuris*) was an act performed before the *comitia curiata,* the assembly organized in the earliest way.[37] One is reminded of the proclamation made at Gortyn in the place of assembly when the citizens had gathered. Again, an early form of will was an act before the *comitia curiata.*[38] But such acts have only antiquarian interest. The procedure prevalent in the classical period, the procedure from which most of the Roman law of bequest developed, was unlike anything practised in Gortyn or Athens. It was an application of the conveyance called *mancipatio per aes et libram.* The testator wrote his wishes on wax tablets. He carried out *mancipatio* of his property to a person called the *familiae emptor* and gave him the tablets. The *familiae emptor* ("purchaser of the estate") may have begun as an executor, but as the procedure developed he became a man of straw. Moreover, this procedure, the mancipatory will, gave rise after a time to an easier form, the praetorian will. Mancipation required the presence of a *libripens* (a man holding a symbolic pair of scales), of the *familiae emptor,* and of five witnesses; these amount to seven persons apart from the testator. So the praetor declared that he would grant "possession of the estate" (*bonorum possessio*) to an heir named in a written document, provided that it was sealed by seven witnesses.[39]

Nothing resembling the rules of the mancipatory will or of the praetorian will is known from any Greek city. Their development springs from the Roman concept of the family. This concept is characterized by the extensive authority of the father (*patria potestas*). This authority was extensive in more than one aspect. Unless the father emancipated a child (or gave a daughter into marriage with *manus,* see below), his authority continued until he died. So a grandfather or great-grandfather, as long as alive, retained authority over his descendants. The descendants were not "independent" (*sui iuris*) but "under authority" (*in potestate*). The

---

37. Nicholas, *Introduction to Roman Law,* 77.
38. Ibid., 253.
39. Gaius 2.102–104, 119–120; Just. *Inst.* 2.10.1–3; Nicholas, *Introduction to Roman Law,* 254–55.

aspect of paternal authority that is relevant here is that property acquired by the descendants belonged to the living male ancestor in the male line (*pater familias*).[40]

The Roman concept of the family is highly patriarchal. Only the living male ancestor is *sui iuris*. As owner of the property he can dispose of it, the conveyance being *mancipatio*. So he can transfer the *familia* to another person, who steps into his legal place and acquires all his rights and duties. Hence he can make a mancipatory will. Consequently, if a will fulfills the conditions for validity, the heir whom it names takes the inheritance and excludes persons who might claim on grounds of kinship. This result contrasts with practice in Athens, for there sons have priority. The contrast arises from a difference in the underlying concept of the family.

Consequences of the difference deserve to be pursued further. When an Athenian boy was in his eighteenth year, his father presented him to the members of his deme. If these were satisfied about his age and parentage, they added him to their list. Inscription on the list of the deme brought all the rights and obligations of citizenship.[41] Once the young men had been enrolled, they underwent two years of military training as ephebes (*ephēboi*). The ephebate as described by Aristotle may have been reformed and made more strict a short time after the battle of Chaironeia, but in some form it existed previously; it was probably old.[42] Compulsory military training of two years between the ages of eighteen and twenty is attested in other parts of Greece, including Sparta, Kyrene, and the cities of Crete.[43] The practice was evidently widespread. There is nowhere any suggestion that a male Greek who had come of age was still subject to his father. A young Athenian might take a wife in deference to his father's wishes, or at least he might say

---

40. Gaius 1.49, 55, 127; 2.86-87; Just. *Inst.* 1.9; Nicholas, *Introduction to Roman Law*, 65-69. It was left to Justinian in the sixth century to modify the rule about acquisition: Just. *Inst.* 2.9.1-2.

41. Ar. *AP.* 42.1. Interpretation of the requirement of age has been clarified by M. Golden, "Demosthenes and the Age of Majority at Athens," *Phoenix* 33 (1979): 25-38.

42. Its existence well before the battle of Chaironeia is known from Aischin. 2.167. On the reform and the later condition see Ar. *AP.* 42; Lyk. fr. 20 (Conomis); *SIG*[3]. 957; cf. F.W. Mitchel, "The So-Called Earliest Ephebic Inscription," *ZPE* 19 (1975): 233-43; C. Pélékidis, *Histoire de l' éphébie attique des origines à 31 avant Jésus-Christ* (Paris: de Boccard, 1962).

43. Sparta: Plut. *Lyk.* 17.2; Kyrene and Crete: Eustathios, *Commentary on Odyssey* 1592.57-58 on *Od.* 8.247; cf. Sealey, *Women and Law*, 55-57.

so in court,[44] but that was a consequence of personal respect, not obedience to authority.

The contrast of concepts can be illustrated further by comparing the Roman kinsmen entitled to inherit *ab intestato* with the degrees of relationship recognized in Athenian law. According to the Twelve Tables, if a Roman died without leaving descendants and without making a will, his property passed to his nearest agnatic relative. If that relative was not available to act, the property passed to the members of the dead man's *gens*.[45]

Agnatic kinship is relationship traced through male ancestors only. People of both sexes can be related agnatically. A man or a woman is an agnatic relative of his or her paternal uncle and of his or her paternal aunt, but one has no agnatic relationship to one's maternal uncle or maternal aunt. In short, agnatic relatives are people who would have been subject to the *patria potestas* of the same known ancestor, if he had lived longer. The *gens* was a group of families who claimed descent in the male line from a common male ancestor, real or legendary, and this tie was reflected in nomenclature.[46] The members of a man's *gens* included his agnatic relatives but were more extensive. The word is often and reasonably translated "clan." Gentilician ties sprang from the highly patriarchal way in which Romans conceived society. The descendants of a common ancestor in the male line were regarded almost as a corporate unit and an element of the state. It has sometimes been conjectured that the Roman family arose from a prehistoric condition, when the kinsmen held the property in common and the *pater familias* was only their representative for the duration of his life.[47] Such a picture, whether it had ever existed in fact or not, may have haunted the minds of those who developed the law, but as early as the time of the Twelve Tables the *pater familias* was an owner who could alienate property by will.

The Athenian rules on intestate succession have already been noted briefly and now require attention in detail. If a man died without leaving descendants or naming an heir by adoption or testament, his inheritance passed

---

44. [Dem.] 40.4, 12.
45. Twelve Tables V, 4–5; cf. Nicholas, *Introduction to Roman Law,* 247–48.
46. The *locus classicus* on the *gens* is Cic. *Top.* 29. Gaius (3.17) remarked that the institution had decayed by his time.
47. H.S. Maine, *Ancient Law* (1861; reprint, London: Dent, 1965), 108–10.

1. to his brothers begotten by the same father and to children of those brothers; but if there were no persons of this kind, it passed
2. to his sisters begotten by the same father and to children of those sisters; but if there were no persons of this kind, it passed
3. to his cousins on his father's side and to children of those cousins; but if there were no persons of this kind, it passed
4. to his relatives on his mother's side in the same order.

Relatives within the stated degrees, that is, relatives as far as cousins and children of cousins, were called *anchisteis*.[48] Relatives defined by this limit had a further function in Athenian law. If a man was killed, these relatives took part in the proclamation that initiated proceedings against the killer.[49] This practice implies that the law recognized relatives within the stated degrees as having a right of revenge, when public authority set about substituting legal proceedings for self-help (a topic to be pursued in chaps. 4 and 5). So the function of the *anchisteis* in response to homicide suggests the idea that led the law to define kinship by this limit. One's *anchisteis* were the people from whom one could expect help in an emergency. In return they had an interest in one's property as eventual heirs.

Anchisteia at Athens plays a part only in the law of homicide and the law of intestate succession. The concepts are wholly different from

---

48. Isai. 11.1-3. Parts of the same order are confirmed by Isai. 7.20, 22. If there were no living *anchisteis*, the inheritance passed to the nearest surviving relative on the father's side: [Dem.] 43.51. Since cousins are included in the order of succession, it is surprising that uncles are not. J.H. Lipsius (*Das attische Recht* und Rechtsverfahren, 3 vols. [Leipzig: Reisland, 1905-15], 555-56 n. 43) reviews previous discussions and argues that uncles were included immediately before cousins; the list of qualified relatives at Isai. 11.1-3 may be incomplete. The argument of Lipsius rests on three texts. (1) At 10.4-5 Isaios indicates that the uncle of an *epiklēros* could claim her for himself or for his son. (2) At 3.63 and 74 Isaios maintains that the uncles of the deceased father of an *epiklēros* could claim her for one of their kinsmen. (3) At Isaios 1.44-45 a nephew claims to inherit from his maternal uncle and says: "I think that you consider yourselves entitled to inherit—and to be aggrieved if you do not inherit—from those who are entitled to inherit from you." This last statement is false; in Athens children inherited from parents but parents did not inherit from children. The argument for including uncles in the reconstructed law of succession rests on the right of an uncle to take an *epiklēros* with her inheritance. But that right may have arisen because her cousin, the uncle's son, was sometimes a minor. The objection to including uncles is that ascendants did not inherit (Lipsius, *Attisches Recht*, 549-50), and if uncles could have inherited, surely parents would have had priority over them.

49. *IG* 1³. 104 = Meiggs and Lewis no. 86, ll. 20-21; cf. [Dem.] 43.57.

those that shaped Roman law on kinship. There is no suggestion at Athens that kinsmen are held together by patriarchal authority; there is no ground to suppose that any prehistoric or notional image of property held in common lingered in the Athenian mind.

The order of intestate succession at Gortyn has already been noticed (at n. 36 above). As at Athens, male persons have priority over females, but females and persons related to the deceased through females are not excluded (the Gortynian and Athenian words translated by *children* embrace both sexes). A further feature of the Gortynian code contrasts with Rome. A section of the code (VI, 2-46) protects the property of members of a family against alienation by other members of the same family. The provisions may be summarized thus:

1. A son is not to alienate property of his father, while the father is alive, but may alienate his own property.
2. A father is not to alienate property of his children.
3. A husband is not to alienate property of his wife, and a son is not to alienate property of his mother. The code supports this prohibition with the sanction against fraud, discussed in chapter 2, and adds a bar against retroactive enforcement.
4. If a woman dies leaving children, their father is to administer her property, but he is not to alienate it unless the children have come of age and give their consent. The sanction against fraud follows. Further, if the father marries another wife, the children of the deceased wife are to administer the property left by their mother.

Evidently the Gortynian concept of the family contrasts with that current in Rome and resembles the Athenian concept. The different members of the family have individual rights to property, even before they come of age. Admittedly the laws recognize that, after someone has died, the heirs may decide to own the property jointly or to divide it between themselves (V, 28-34, 44-54). But that was a matter of free choice.

Women

The same lines of contrast and resemblance appear in the law of marriage and dowry. At Rome a woman could be given into "marriage with *manus*." That is, she was removed from the *patria potestas* of her father (or of his *pater familias*) and came under the authority of her husband (or of his *pater familias*). The new authority was called *manus* and cannot be distinguished in substance from *patria potestas*. In particular, any property acquired by the woman belonged to her husband (or to his *pater familias*), and when he died, she received a daughter's share in the inheritance.[50] Marriage with *manus* could be brought about by *coemptio*, which was an application of *mancipatio per aes et libram*. But ownership of property could be acquired through that conveyance or by prescription (*usus*), the periods being one year for movables and two years for immovables. So marital authority over a woman could be acquired by prescription of one year; that is, if the man and the woman lived together continuously for a year, the woman passed from the paternal authority of her original family to the *manus* of her husband. The early rule about dowry followed from these principles. Any dowry supplied by the woman's original family was owned henceforth by her husband or his *pater familias*.[51]

Under certain conditions marriage could come about "without *manus*."[52] The woman then retained her previous status; she might be subject to the authority of her own *pater familias*, or if he had died or emancipated her, she would be independent (*sui iuris*). Marriage without *manus* became common in the Late Republic, and so did divorce. So the praetors created an action (the *actio rei uxoriae*) to enable the wife, under some conditions concerning children and fault, to recover the dowry if the marriage was terminated by divorce or death of the husband.[53]

At Athens a woman needed a man as her *kyrios*. He can be regarded as her guardian, or as her master, and in particular as administrator of her property, for she could not herself carry out a transaction in a value exceeding a medimnos of barley (see chap. 1 at n. 33). This restriction dominated the law of marriage. The procedure best attested consisted in two acts, *engyēsis* and *ekdosis*. The former was a betrothal but may be called "a strong betrothal." It is often mentioned in speeches on issues of marriage and inheritance, although whether it was actionable is not

---

50. Gaius 1.108–10; 2.86; 3.3; Nicholas, *Introduction to Roman Law*, 82.
51. Nicholas, *Introduction to Roman Law*, 88.
52. The Twelve Tables (VI, 5) provided that a woman did not come under the authority of her husband if she stayed away from his house for three nights in the year. By the time of Cicero additional methods had been devised for achieving this result; see A. Watson, *The Law of Persons in the Later Roman Republic* (Oxford: Oxford University Press, 1967), 19–31.
53. Nicholas, *Introduction to Roman Law*, 88; Watson, *Law of Persons*, 57–76.

known. Evidently it was a significant part of the process of transferring *kyrieia* over the woman from the representative of her original family, often her father, to the bridegroom. *Ekdosis* followed as the physical transfer of the woman to her new dwelling.

The man who gave a woman into engyetic marriage uttered a set form of words, and in doing so he specified a dowry.[54] The dowry, called *proix,* must be distinguished from the woman's personal belongings or paraphernalia, called "cloaks and gold jewelry" (*himatia kai chrysia*), although they might include many things, even slaves for attendance on the woman. The dowry was a sum of money, or things on which a monetary value was set in agreement with the bridegroom. The revenues from the dowry were intended for the woman's maintenance. If the husband fell into debt, his creditors could seize his property, but they could be excluded from property that was shown to be his wife's dowry.[55] If she bore children and then died, her sons inherited the dowry.[56] If the marriage was dissolved, the woman returned to her original family and its head became her *kyrios* again. The divorced husband was required to return the dowry. If he failed to do so, the woman's relatives had a remedy called significantly the *dikē sitou* or "action for grain," and they could exact interest at a rate determined by law.[57] As long as the marriage lasted, the husband had authority to administer the dowry, and if he misused it, the only recourse was divorce. But the husband did not own the dowry, since it could be protected against his creditors if he fell into debt. Whether the woman herself owned the dowry is a question of definition and need not be pursued here. It has been well said that the dowry of an Athenian woman came into being at her birth; it was her claim on her father's property for support.[58]

At Rome marriage with *manus* extinguished the rights and obligations previously in force between the woman and her original *pater familias*.

---

54. For the set form of words see n. 4 above. *Engyēsis* and *proix* have been clarified in many previous studies. The outstanding ones are H.J. Wolff, "Marriage Law and Family Organization in Ancient Athens: A Study in the Interrelation of Public and Private Law in the Greek City," *Traditio* 2 (1944): 43-95, and idem, "*Proix,*" *RE* 23:133-70. The subjects are treated in standard handbooks, for example, Harrison, *Family,* 1-60.

55. [Dem.] 47.57; cf. Dem. 30.8.

56. Sealey, *Women and Law,* 27-28, arguing from comparison of Dem. 36.14-15, 32, with 45.28. If there was a daughter and the father died, the sons inherited the obligation to provide her a dowry out of their total assets.

57. [Dem.] 59.52; Isai. 3.9.

58. I thank Mr. Richard Sterling for pointing this out to me.

She became wholly a member of her husband's family and was said to be "in the place of a daughter" to him.[59] Marriage without *manus* had no effect on the personal status of the woman. If she was independent (*sui iuris*), she remained so, and if she was in the *potestas* of her *pater familias,* she remained so. In Athens, on the other hand, marriage transferred authority (*kyrieia*) over the woman from the head of her original family to her husband. Consequently, the legal relationship between the woman and her original family was put into abeyance, but it revived in full force if the marriage was terminated by divorce or by death of the husband. Athenian practice attached importance to the contract of betrothal (*engyēsis*) because it was the first step in transferring *kyrieia*. A contract of betrothal (*sponsalia*) may have been known in Rome at an early date, but by 200 B.C. it had ceased to be actionable and was merely a social convention.[60] The different development in the procedures for contracting marriage is not primary. The fundamental difference between Romans and Athenians is an underlying difference of substance in beliefs about marriage and about the legal capacity of women.

At Gortyn no words equivalent to *engyēsis* or *proix* are attested. As already observed, the laws have a lengthy section about marrying the *patrōiōkos,* the heiress or female orphan (VII, 15 to IX, 24), but they do not say how any other woman is to be married. Yet the rules about the heiress include a provision to be followed "if a woman who has been given by her father or brother becomes a *patrōiōkos*" (VIII, 20-22). It follows that a woman could be given into marriage by her father or brother, as long as one of those relatives was alive. The allusion to the woman given thus into marriage does not exclude the possibility that marriage might be contracted in yet a third way; perhaps a woman who was not a *patrōiōkos* could enter into marriage otherwise than by an act of her father or brother.[61] But there is no positive reason to suppose a third mode of marriage.

Although the law-code has no word for dowry, it has a good deal to say about property owned by women. Children have an interest in the property of both their parents, since they will inherit it, a daughter's share being half of a son's share (with some restrictions, IV, 31-48). If someone is condemned by a court to make a payment, he may take his eventual share in the parental property at once for that purpose. With

---

59. Gaius 3.3.
60. Watson, *Law of Persons,* 11-18.
61. I thank Mr. David Silverman for drawing my attention to this possibility.

that exception, the parents, as long as they are alive, may retain the property, or, if they wish, they may hand it over to the children (IV, 23-31). A father may give to his daughter at marriage or previously property in an amount not exceeding her eventual share in his inheritance. (IV, 48 to V, 1).

From these rules it appears that the Gortynian woman, like the Athenian woman, can be given into marriage and can bring property with her, but it is limited in amount to her eventual share in her paternal inheritance. Let it be supposed that a marriage has thus come about. Gifts made by a husband to his wife, or by a son to his mother, are not to exceed one hundred staters (X, 14-20). This restriction is followed at once by a rule that declares invalid any gifts made by a debtor until he has satisfied his creditors (X, 20-25). So the purpose of the restriction to one hundred staters may be to prevent a debtor from defrauding his creditors by gifts to his wife or mother. If a marriage is dissolved, the woman is to have "her own property, which she had when she went to the man," half of the proceeds from that property, and half of anything she has produced during the marriage (II, 45-54). A similar principle is to be observed if the marriage is terminated through the death of the husband. The woman is to have her own property, half of the proceeds from it, and any gifts that the man gave her within the legal restriction; if the marriage has already born children, the woman is free to marry or not to marry again, as she wishes (III, 17-31). If, on the other hand the marriage is terminated through the death of the woman and there are no children, her blood relations as heirs are to receive her property, half of the proceeds from it, and half of anything she has produced during the marriage (III, 31-37).

So far the provisions are much like those governing the dowry of an Athenian woman. At Gortyn, as at Athens, a woman brings property with her into marriage. This property is called dowry in Athens and the woman's property in Gortyn. That is a mere difference of wording; at Athens sons who had inherited their deceased mother's dowry could call it "the maternal property."[62] At Athens the amount of the dowry was at the discretion of the man who gave the woman into marriage, but at Gortyn it was limited to her share in the eventual inheritance. At Athens in consequence of divorce the woman took her dowry back to her original family. The Gortynian lawgiver has thought further; he provides that

---

62. Dem. 36.32, cf. 14-15.

on divorce the woman shall recover the property that she brought with her into the marriage, half of the proceeds from it, and half of anything she herself has made. These differences do not amount to much. It should not be forgotten that laws distributing property among rival claimants are essentially guidelines; in any actual case the parties are likely to negotiate.

Attention must also be paid to administration of the woman's property while the marriage lasts. Note was taken above (p. 76) of rules protecting the property of members of the family against alienation by other members of the same family (VI, 2-46). A sanction was added to protect the property of a woman against alienation by her husband or son, and the sanction was accompanied by a provision against retroactive enforcement (VI, 9-25). No explicit sanction was stated to uphold the prohibitions of alienation of the father's property by the son and of the son's property by the father. Evidently the lawgiver had to take greater care to protect the property of wives and mothers. That is, the husband or the son had actual opportunity to alienate the property of the wife or the mother. The bar against retroactive enforcement does not necessarily mean that the rule now upheld was wholly new; it may imply that previous practice had varied, or that the rule had been uncertain. At least the bar implies that previously husbands and sons had sometimes alienated property of their women effectively. The sanction and the bar together show that husbands and sons could administer the property of their wives and mothers. In other words they behaved like the Athenian *kyrios*.

Another feature reflects similarity between Athens and Gortyn in the relation of women to property. At Athens a law provided explicitly that a child or a woman could not engage in a transaction in greater value than a medimnos of barley. From this the inference was drawn in an extant speech that a child could not make a will. It could also be inferred that a woman could not make a will.[63] The code of Gortyn says:

Neither a woman nor a person under age shall adopt. (XI, 18-19)

Thus spokesmen for both cities associate women with children in a common restriction on their powers over property. Athenians were Ionian, Gortynians were Dorian. The two cities were far apart. They

---

63. Isai. 10.10. The inference about testamentary incapacity of women is confirmed by the attempt of Archippe to distribute her dowry in unequal parts and by its failure: Sealey, *Women and Law,* 27-28.

differed markedly in size and prosperity. Yet on some matters concerning women and property Athenians and Gortynians thought the same thoughts.

Many aspects of Greek authority over women (*kyrieia*) have already been noted, and not much more need be said. Inscriptions of Hellenistic date from many parts of the Greek area, though not from Athens, show women performing major transactions in property. Sometimes the collaboration of a *kyrios* is mentioned, sometimes it is not.[64] An attractive illustration, which will require note in another context, is the will made by Epikteta at Thera in the third century B.C.[65] The will creates a cult of the testator's husband and sons, who had all died, and prospectively of herself. The opening lines say that the will was made by Epikteta "with her *kyrios*." He was her son-in-law. In the same circumstances an Athenian woman too came under the *kyrieia* of her son-in-law. The condition of Epikteta differed from that of an Athenian woman in that she could make a will. But in her subjection to *kyrieia* she resembled the Athenian woman.

In general, when an inscription records a transaction performed by a woman but does not mention a *kyrios,* one cannot infer that no *kyrios* took part. An inscription does not record all aspects of a transaction but only the aspects that the inscriber wished to proclaim. Again, even if the collaboration of a *kyrios* is mentioned, one cannot tell whether he exercised an effective restriction on the woman's freedom or merely carried out a formality of ratification. Even so, a conclusion of some importance emerges about the authority exercised over a Greek woman. It could be exercised by different people according to her changing familial circumstances. Her *kyrios* might be her father, her brother, her grandfather, or her uncle; in consequence of marriage her *kyrios* would be her husband or eventually her adult son or son-in-law. But in any one city at any one time the degree of authority exercised by the *kyrios,* whoever he might be, was uniform. A Greek woman was subject to *kyrieia* solely because she was a woman.

Rome provides a sharp contrast. In consequence of birth a Roman woman, like a man, was subject to the extensive *potestas* of her father (or of his *pater familias*). In consequence of marriage she might or might not become subject to the *manus* of her husband, and *manus* was similar

---

64. Cf. T.W. Beasley, "The *Kyrios* in Greek States Other Than Athens," *CR* 20 (1906): 249–53.

65. *IG* 12. 3, 330.

in extent to *patria potestas*. But if she was emancipated by her *pater familias,* or if the person exercising *potestas* or *manus* over her died, she became independent (*sui iuris*). Once she was independent, she could own property. She was subject to the authority (*tutela*) of a *tutor,* but this was authority of a much milder kind. In its earliest form, *tutela legitima,* it was exercised by her nearest agnatic relative. He was her eventual heir. The nearest agnatic relative was also *tutor* to an orphaned male child, but the *tutela* ceased when the male child grew up. The cessation of *tutela* over males is the clue to explaining its continuation over females. The effect of *tutela* was merely that the person subject to it could not alienate property without the consent of the *tutor* (so it is misleading to translate *tutor* as "guardian," a word suggesting authority over the person as well as over property). The *tutor* was the eventual heir. When a male child grew up, he could beget children who on agnatic principles would displace the *tutor* from the inheritance; so *tutela* ceased. But the children of a woman were not agnatically related to her father, and so they could not inherit the patrimony. The authority of the *tutor* over a woman was nothing more than his interest in her property. As time passed, Roman jurists developed *tutela* so as to increase female freedom, until the *tutor*'s share in a woman's transactions was a mere formality of ratification.[66] In Rome, unlike Greece, there was no uniform type of authority to which a woman was subject in consequence of the sole fact that she was a woman.

The Female Orphan

The remaining institution requiring attention in the law of the family is the *epiklēros*. In its Athenian form it was introduced in chapter 1. It is attested elsewhere, for example, at Thera. The will of Epikteta specified the people entitled to take part in the cult that it founded. They included male descendants permanently together with their wives and sons. Daughters could take part only until they were given in marriage, but there was an exception to this restriction. *Epiklēroi* were entitled to take part in perpetuity and so were their husbands and children. Thus the will reflects principles of marriage familiar from Athens. An *epiklēros* belongs permanently to her original family and perpetuates it in her

---

66. Twelve Tables V, 1, 2, 6; Gaius 1.144-45, 192; cf. Watson, *Law of Persons,* 19-31, 102-13, 146-54; Sealey, *Women and Law,* 103-6.

descendants. Other women pass at marriage out of their original family; they become members of the husband's family, which is created by the marriage, and they remain members of it for the duration of the marriage.

At Gortyn the word for the heiress or female orphan is *patrōiōkos*. That is the word, modified in dialect and spelling, which Herodotos uses in talking of Sparta.[67] But although the word differs, the thing is the same. For the law-code of Gortyn states the definition:

> A woman is to be *patrōiōkos* if she has no father or brother begotten by the same father. (VIII, 40–42)

The code provides lengthy rules for assigning the *patrōiōkos* in marriage (VII, 15 to IX, 24). The initial principle is the same as in Athens: the heiress is to be taken in marriage by the man who, as nearest relative of her dead father, succeeds to the property. But the Gortynian lawgiver has provided for many further eventualities: the heir who is entitled to marry the woman may be too young to marry, or the woman may be too young, or the heir may be unwilling to marry her, or he may be out of the country, or there may be no heirs within the recognized degrees of kinship, or again the *patrōiōkos* may be unwilling to marry the heir, or he may be too young and she may be unwilling to wait. In foreseeing the last two eventualities the lawgiver has accorded recognition to female volition, but the recognition is far from generous. If the *patrōiōkos* is unwilling to marry the heir or unwilling to wait until he is old enough for marriage, she forfeits half of her property to him and is married to the suitor of her choice from men of her tribe (VII, 52 to VIII, 8). Admittedly practice could conceivably exploit that provision to such an extent that *patrōiōkoi* would usually choose their husbands. But there is no way of telling whether any such development occurred, and the assumption from which the laws proceeded is the same as in Athens. The female orphan, having no father or brother to care for her interests, is an anomaly and the law must provide for marrying her off.

This assumption is peculiar to Greeks. As noted in chapter 1, at Rome a man or a woman became *sui iuris* on the death of male ascendants and could therefore own property. Roman law did not care whether an independent female person married or did not marry. Critics, however, have objected that the Greek institution is not unique but is paralleled

---

67. *Patrouchos:* Hdt. 6.57.4. But Aristotle (*Pol.* 2.1270a24–29) calls her *epiklēros*.

in the levirate marriage of Hebrew law.⁶⁸ So the latter institution demands attention.

The law on levirate marriage is stated in Deuteronomy 25.5-10:

> When brethren dwell together, and one of them dieth without children, the wife of the deceased shall not marry to another: but his brother shall take her, and raise up seed for his brother. And the first son he shall have of her he shall call by his name: that his name be not abolished out of Israel. But if he will not take his brother's wife, who by law belongeth to him, the woman shall go to the gate of the city, and call upon the ancients, and say: "My husband's brother refuseth to raise up his brother's name in Israel: and will not take me to wife." And they shall cause him to be sent for forthwith, and shall ask him. If he answer: "I will not take her to wife," the woman shall come to him before the ancients, and shall take off his shoe from his foot, and spit in his face, and say: "So shall it be done to the man that will not build up his brother's house." And his name shall be called in Israel "The house of the unshod."⁶⁹

There is an allusion to the institution early in the Book of Ruth. Noemi, whose husband and two sons have died, advises her daughters-in-law to leave her in hope of marrying new husbands elsewhere. For, she observes, she herself is old and not likely to bear more sons; even if she did so, the daughters-in-law now bereft would have to wait many years until the sons would be old enough to marry them (1.11-13). Here Noemi assumes that her future sons, if she had any, would be obliged to marry her widowed daughters-in-law. But the later part of the story, culminating in the marriage of Ruth and Booz, draws mainly on a different institution, a right of redemption (*geʾulla*). By this, if a branch of a family has fallen into poverty, a kinsman from another branch takes its assets (and its obligations) rather than leaving them to its creditors.⁷⁰

---

68. I am indebted to Professors David Cohen and Charles Donahue, Jr., for discussing these ideas with me. They are not to blame for any deficiency in my presentation of their criticism.

69. Douay version. For my understanding of levirate marriage I am indebted to D. Daube, "*Consortium* in Roman and Hebrew Law," *Juridical Review* (Edinburgh) 62 (1950): 71-91, at 71-81. On the survival of the institution into the Middle Ages see W. Pakter, *Medieval Canon Law and the Jews* (Ebelsbach: Gremer, 1988), 251.

70. Ruth 3.9-13; 4.1-13; see W. McKane, "Ruth and Boaz," Glasgow University Oriental Society: *Transactions* 19 (1961-62): 29-40.

The story of Juda and Thamar in Genesis 38 is valuable toward understanding the rules about levirate marriage. Juda had three sons. He secured Thamar as wife for his eldest son. But the eldest son died. So Juda said to his second son: "Go in to thy brother's wife and marry her, that thou mayst raise seed to thy brother" (38.8). The second son avoided this obligation by a subterfuge and suffered death as divine punishment. Juda sent Thamar back to her father's house to wait until his third son should grow up. But even when the third son had done so, Juda did not reclaim Thamar for him, and the story had a romantic outcome, which is of no concern here. The story presupposes a highly patriarchal family, where the father can order his son to marry a woman whom the father has chosen. The law given in Deuteronomy and quoted above says nothing about the situation obtaining while the father is alive. For the father's authority is powerful enough to achieve the desired result without legislation.

When, however, the father dies, the law steps in to assert an obligation. It operates only if the brothers hold their paternal inheritance in common ("when brethren dwell together"). For if they do, the surviving brother (or brothers) might take the whole inheritance for himself and his descendants. Then the line of the deceased brother would come to an end and his widow would be destitute, for as widow she had no right of succession. To avoid these consequences the law requires the surviving brother to marry the widow of the deceased brother.

The levirate marriage of Hebrew law differs in some particular respects from the Greek institution of the *epiklēros:*

1. If the Hebrew brother-in-law does not marry the widow, she can take action at law to bring him into disgrace. The law provides a sanction against him because marrying the widow can be burdensome to him. But for that obligation, he could take the whole property inherited from his father and transmit it to descendants of himself and his original wife. In the Greek practice the male heir does not have to be incited by a sanction, for he gains the benefit of administering the estate and therefore drawing on its proceeds, until the children of himself and the *epiklēros* grow up.
2. The Hebrew rule comes into operation only if the brothers hold their inherited property jointly. The Greek institution has nothing to do with joint ownership.
3. The Hebrew rule presupposes a highly patriarchal condition, where

the father selects a wife for his son. Possibly a similar condition existed among Greeks at a prehistoric period, but if it did, it has left no trace in Greek law. Even if it existed at an early time, it had no formative or lasting effect.

Apart from particular differences, there is an overall difference of major extent between the two institutions. A Hebrew woman becomes a candidate for levirate marriage because her husband has died leaving her without children. A Greek woman becomes *epiklēros* (or *patrōiōkos*) because her father has died leaving her without brothers. The two laws deal with wholly different predicaments. The modern mind, accustomed to female choice as a legally recognized factor in marriage, may see a distant resemblance between the two institutions, because in both the law assigns a woman into marriage and specifies the person who is to take her. No resemblance is apparent from the point of view of societies where male relatives give women in marriage and the law pays no heed to female choice.

The Greek Peculiarity

Thus the institution of the *epiklēros* (or *patrōiōkos*) is wholly Greek. This chapter has recognized distinctively Greek ideas in many features of the law of the family. Testamentary bequest developed among Greeks from the legal fiction of adoption, but in Rome, although adoption was practised, the mancipatory will and therefore the praetorian will became possible because the rights of the *pater familias* embraced his descendants and the property they acquired. In Athens intestate succession was accorded to the *anchisteis,* the relatives on both sides from whom one might expect help, and in Gortyn likewise property was inherited by kinsmen related to the deceased both through male and through female persons, whereas the agnatic kinship of Roman law was grounded in recognition of a patriarch. Roman marriage with *manus* upheld the authority of the patriarch over the family to which the woman was admitted. Greek marriage, on the other hand, did not extinguish the relationship of a woman to her original family but made it latent for the duration of the marriage; marriage by *engyēsis* was rather like a protracted loan of a woman to her husband, whereas Roman marriage by *coemptio* employed a conveyance modeled on sale.

In negative terms, one may say that the distinctive concepts of Greek law lack the Roman preoccupation with patriarchal authority. In positive terms, the adult male Greek had greater freedom than his Roman counterpart. He might have to undertake two years of military training, but that was merely a matter of public law. In private law he was fully independent of his father and ancestors. He owned any property he acquired. He was master of his own *oikos,* even though his sons and contingently his other relatives had rights of inheritance. In short, Greek law in places as different as Athens and Gortyn is uniform in its individualism; the adult male citizen is the characteristic bearer of rights and obligations. In shunning patriarchal concepts Greek law differs not only from Roman concepts but also from Hebrew institutions, of which one illustration has been noticed.

The freedom of the adult male citizen in Greece is reflected by contrast in the underprivileged status of two other categories of persons. One of them is women. Since the Greek woman was not an adult male citizen, she needed such a person to attend to her interests. This is certainly true of cities where *kyrieia* is attested. It is probably true also of Gortyn. Reason was found to believe that the husband or son often administered the property of a married woman there, and the rules about the *patrōiōkos* imply that the female orphan was an anomaly, as in Athens, since she had no father or brother to assign her in marriage. At Rome, on the other hand, the extensive authority of the *pater familias* created a basis of equality among his descendants of both sexes, and the disabilities of women, consequent on birth into a highly patriarchal family, challenged jurists to liberate them in developing the law.

The other underprivileged category was aliens. Athenian citizens were conscious of their own superiority to metics. They expected them to behave well, they tolerated metics, and they rewarded some of them with individual grants of privileges. The immigrant was in no better condition than a former slave who had been manumitted. In Rome on the other hand formal manumission conferred citizenship. Accordingly citizenship in Rome was a less elevated status than in Greece and could be granted to many strangers, including whole communities. Greek cities tended to guard their citizenship jealously, especially in the classical period. Greek thought on social relations was guided by a concept of the fully privileged member of the community. This concept appears in the legal systems of more than one city. It may well be the underlying idea that gave rise to the features common to different cities, features that amount to a degree of unity in Greek law, even though at the superficial level different cities developed different rules. Moreover, the concept of the fully privileged member of the community may, in view of its broad import, lie at the root of the Greek contribution to justice, and therefore a later chapter (6) will ask where this concept came from. But first something must be said about procedural elements in Greek law.

CHAPTER 4

How to Resolve Disputes I: Greece

Elements of homogeneity in the legal systems of different Greek cities were recognized in the previous chapter. In addition to particular similarities, the concept of the fully privileged member of the community was singled out, not merely because it was common to different cities but also because it was a dynamic idea such as could direct the development of law. In chapter 2 the emergence of codes of law was studied and it was suggested that these developed from earlier practices of adjudicating disputes. Once a court of whatever kind exists, it may resolve specific disputes. The court or a person who is to serve in the court may advance from settling disputes between named persons to enunciating generalized principles in casuistic formulation ("if anyone does such and such a thing..."). This and the next chapter will scrutinize Greek procedures for settling disputes. In chapter 6 it may finally become possible to discern a causal connection between those procedures and the idea of the fully privileged member of the community.

For a start, let it be supposed that two men have a dispute. Each of them believes himself entitled to one and the same thing. Perhaps one of them possesses the thing and the other claims it from him. Their dispute may lead them to fight, or each may call out his sympathizers in the hope of overcoming or overawing the other. Again, a third person may intervene and try to mediate a settlement at the request of the parties or on his own initiative, if he hopes to prevent a fight. Yet it may happen that none of these informal modes of settlement is acceptable to one or both parties, or some of them may be attempted and fail. Then the parties go to court.

But suppose that there are no courts. Philosophers of the seventeenth and eighteenth centuries thought that such a condition had once existed;

they called it "the state of nature." Whether that condition had ever existed is a question that need not be pursued here. It may still be profitable to imagine a state of nature in order to discover the essential character of a court. Homer comes to the aid of the imagination. He describes a dispute between Menelaos and Antilochos for the second prize in the chariot race, which was among the competitions held at the funeral of Patroklos. The dispute was resolved without violence.[1]

Menelaos and Antilochos

The chariot race had five competitors and plentiful excitement. For a time Eumelos was likely to win. But the pole of his chariot broke; according to the poet, who had superior knowledge, it was broken by Athena. She also restored to Diomedes the whip that he had dropped, or rather Apollo had snatched it from him. At any rate Diomedes came in first and received the first prize, a woman and a tripod. Eumelos, dragging his disabled chariot and driving his horses, came in last of the five competitors, but Achilles offered him the second prize, a mare, and the Achaians approved. Antilochos, however, did not approve. He claimed the second prize because he had come in second. Achilles yielded to the force of this argument, gave the mare to Antilochos, and gave Eumelos a thorax of bronze in consolation.

At this point the dispute for the second prize began. Menelaos had come in close behind Antilochos. He was aggrieved. The course had led through a place where the path was narrow, because on one side the ground had fallen away. Here Antilochos had urged his horses ahead recklessly and Menelaos had held back to avoid a collision. At the moment when Antilochos thus drove ahead of him, Menelaos exclaimed that Antilochos would not get the prize "without an oath" (23.441). Evidently Menelaos and the Greek audience listening to the *Iliad* could expect a dispute and a resolution of the dispute by means of an oath.

When Achilles assigned the mare to Antilochos, Menelaos complained in a speech of moderate length (23.570–85). Early in the speech he invited the leaders of the Argives to provide a *dikē* (*dikassate,* 574). A few lines later he added:

> But come, I myself will provide a *dikē,* and I maintain that no other

---

1. *Il.* 23.566–600. Toward understanding how the dispute is resolved I am indebted to G. Thür, "Zum *dikazein* bei Homer," *ZSR* 87 (1970): 426–44.

of the Danaans will find fault with me. For my *dikē* will be straight. (579-80)

From these utterances it follows that a *dikē* is not a judgment such as can only be given by a third person wielding authority. The *dikē* desired by Menelaos may be provided by a third person or by one of the parties, such as Menelaos himself.[2] But although a *dikē* is not a judgment, it brings the dispute nearer to resolution. So far one cannot tell whether a *dikē* is a settlement or a step toward a settlement.

Menelaos continued and concluded his speech thus:

Antilochos, cherished of Zeus, come hither, as is lawful (*themis*), stand in front of thy horses and thy chariot, hold in thy hands the pliant whip, with which thou drovest previously the horses, and touching the horses swear by the earth-encompassing Lord of Earthquakes that thou didst not voluntarily impede my chariot by a trick. (581-85)

In short Menelaos undertook to provide a *dikē,* and following up this undertaking he formulated an oath that he invited Antilochos to swear. But Antilochos did not swear the oath. Instead he expressed respect for the more advanced age of Menelaos. He apologized for the foolishness of his youth, and he gave Menelaos the mare. At that Menelaos was so mollified that he replied in equally courteous language and restored the mare to Antilochos (600-613). But this response of Menelaos has no bearing on the procedure followed in settling the dispute.

That procedure consisted in formulating an oath of denial for one party to swear. Before formulating it, Menelaos said that his *dikē* would be straight. In archaic Greek a good *dikē* is commonly said to be straight and a bad one is crooked. But when Menelaos, conducting proceedings in his own cause, said that his *dikē* would be straight, it does not necessarily follow that an impartial third person would apply that epithet to the terms formulated for the oath. In the speech of surrender, Antilochos did not talk about the respective merits of the two claims but about the age of Menelaos and the folly of his own youth. In Homeric society relative age is among the factors enabling a man to win a following in his community. That is, age with its supposed wisdom is one of the

---

2. Cf. M. Gagarin, "Dike in the *Works and Days,*" *CP* 68 (1973): 81-94.

factors in political power. The procedure initiated by Menelaos gave Antilochos the opportunity to estimate the relative power that he and his adversary wielded among the bystanders. So he gave up his claim.

The god by whom Antilochos was invited to swear was Poseidon. He was appropriate because he was powerful and he concerned himself with horses. Toward understanding the procedure two features call for comment. One is the wording of the proposed oath and the other is the role of oaths in Homeric thought.

Voluntarily

Menelaos invited Antilochos to swear that he had not done something voluntarily. A recent and thorough study of his word, *hekōn* ("voluntary, voluntarily"), and its correlate, *akōn* ("involuntary, involuntarily"), has clarified their force.[3] These words occur in statements reporting the deed of an agent or the suffering of a victim. The two words attribute contrasting attitudes to the agent or the victim. To say that an agent or a victim did or experienced something *hekōn* is to say that he accepted the deed or the experience as his own. The agent who acted *hekōn* committed himself fully to the deed, and the victim who underwent an experience *hekōn* accepted the suffering. The contrasting word, *akōn*, dissociates the agent or victim from the deed or the experience. To say that someone did something *akōn* is to divorce him from the act. The essential difference is between the commitment of an agent or victim to an occurrence and his divorcement from it.

It can be added that an agent's divorcement from his act could be expressed in other words. As a boy Patroklos killed another boy "not intentionally (*ethelōn*), in anger over a game of bones" (*Il*. 23.88). Patently an agent who regrets a deed may distance himself from it in varying degrees and by various words. Patently also the divorcement of an agent from his deed and the degrees of that divorcement raise an unlimited question for judicial inquiry, but the inquiry cannot be avoided, once

---

3. G. Rickert, *Hekōn and Akōn in Early Greek Thought* (American Classical Studies 20, Atlanta: Scholars Press, 1989). The main finding is stated briefly on p. 128: "In effect, *hekōn* and *akōn* express the agent's or victim's attitude toward what is happening: if *hekōn*, a strong positive attitude or commitment; if *akōn*, a strong negative attitude or divorcement." One can sympathize with the author's inclusion of the word *early* in the title of her book, but she rightly includes plentiful material from authors of the high classical period, such as Euripides. Once adopted, the idea expressed by the two contrasting words was likely to be kept.

people have recognized that an agent's attitude to his deed should modify the consequences for him. The Athenians distinguished between voluntary and involuntary homicide. At Rome the Twelve Tables (VIII, 10) distinguished between the man who set fire to another man's house or barn *sciens prudensque* and the man who did so *casu*. Germanic law from its earliest known stages distinguished between intentional and unintentional misdeeds. The law presumed that the deed was intentional and it assigned to the agent the burden of proving otherwise, but it allowed him various ways of accomplishing this. In some systems, for example, after the victim had opened proceedings, the accused agent could swear that he had not intended harm.[4]

An assertion that a deed was unintentional differs in logical status, according as it is made in the third or the first person. The agent has an interest in divorcing himself from his misdeed. In diplomatic circumstances his words of divorcement may even amount to nothing more than an expression of regret. But when Menelaos tendered an oath to Antilochos, the formulation was highly significant. He laid weight on the word "(not) voluntarily," by placing it at the beginning of the proposed oath and straight after the imperative, "swear," and by marking it off with a particle, *men*. Later in the phrase he inserted the word "by a trick" in specifying the deed of Antilochos. In this way Menelaos denied his adversary any opportunity to raise the question, whether his deed amounted to trickery. Had an impartial third person inquired into the dispute, he might have focused on the question, whether Antilochos had behaved improperly in pushing ahead into the narrow part of the course, in short, whether the deed was trickery. The merits of the rival claims to the second prize depended on that question. The formulation of the oath by Menelaos was thus tendentious. But the purpose of the procedure that he initiated and Antilochos followed was not to weigh the relative merits of the rival claims to the second prize. The purpose was to bring the dispute to an end without bloodshed.

Homeric Oaths

Many oaths are sworn in the *Iliad* and the *Odyssey*, and they sometimes play a part in major public events, such as the reconciliation of

---

4. K. von Amira and K.A. Eckhardt, *Germanisches Recht,* vol. 2 (Berlin: de Gruyter, 1967), 126–29.

Agamemnon and Achilles. To avoid importing extraneous assumptions it is proper to ask, what is an oath?, and what is a Greek oath? Greek treaties of the classical period exemplify oaths consisting of three elements.[5] There is first an invocation; the person swearing the oath names some gods. The second element is the content of the oath; the person swearing says that he will observe the treaty. Third, there is an imprecation, often in the form: "If I keep my oath, may I experience many good things, but if I prove to have sworn falsely, may I experience the opposite."

It is not necessarily to be assumed that Homeric oaths will conform to the pattern known from classical treaties. Every society has its own type or types of oath. At Rome in the *legis actio sacramento* the oath was a wager. Each party declared himself willing to lose a sum of money if his assertion of right to the thing in dispute was not true; the sum was fifty *asses* or five hundred *asses,* according to the value of the thing in dispute. The one party said to the other: "Since thou hast claimed wrongfully, I challenge thee by oath (*sacramento*) at fifty *asses,*" and the other replied: "And I thee." The party who then lost the case paid the sum wagered to the state.[6] This oath resembles that known to Greek treaties in that it has an element equivalent to imprecation; the person swearing undertakes to lose fifty *asses* (or five hundred *asses*) if his claim is not true. But the oath of the *legis actio* differs because it lacks an invocation; no gods are drawn into the procedure. Likewise early Germanic law knew a procedure for settling disputes by oath in which a party offered valuables, undertaking to surrender them if his claim was not true. This oath did not necessarily include an invocation; a god was only invoked if the valuables were eventually to be taken from the losing party by the god.[7]

In approaching Homeric oaths one may watch for the three elements

---

5. Some or all of the elements are illustrated in each of the following documents: Meiggs and Lewis no. 47, lines 42-55; Tod no. 127, lines 16-38; no. 142, lines 58-81; no. 158, lines 5-6; Andok. 1.97-98.

6. Gaius 4.13-14, 16. It must be admitted that some have declined to call the *sacramentum* of the *legis actio* an oath and have supposed that it was originally a sacrifice (for brief discussion and references see J. Gaudemet, *Institutions de l' antiquité* [Paris: Sirey, 1967], 411-12). But it is better to extend the concept of oath. For even if the *legis actio sacramento* originated from sacrifice, it continued to be used and understood after that origin had been forgotten.

7. Amira and Eckhardt, *Germanisches Recht,* 2:166-72.

of invocation, content, and imprecation, although one should not necessarily assume that they will all be present or that they will appear in familiar forms. One may start from an oath where the accompanying gestures are specified. At the bidding of Hypnos, Hera swore to give him Pasithea to wife. She swore by the river Styx. She put one hand on the earth and the other on the sea, so that the lower gods would be witnesses (*martyroi*), and she promised to give Pasithea to Hypnos (*Il.* 14.270-80). In this oath no imprecation is stated. The content is the promise made by Hera. The invocation is elaborate, for it includes gestures with the hands and reference to the Styx and the lower gods.

Homeric oaths often invoke gods. Sometimes the name of a god or gods is introduced with the word *istō:* "Let such and such a god know."[8] Hypnos expressed the same idea when he exacted an oath from Hera and spoke of the lower gods as prospective witnesses.[9] Occasionally in the invocation the name of a god is introduced with the particle *ma*.[10] Some importance attaches to oaths in which the invocation is addressed not to a god but to a thing. Achilles swears by the scepter and expatiates on its significance; the sons of the Achaians hold it in their hands when they administer justice.[11] Sometimes a thing is coupled with a god or gods in the invocation. When Hera swears to Zeus she invokes their bed as well as a series of gods.[12] Telemachos swears by Zeus and by the sufferings of his father.[13] More than one person invokes in his oath Zeus, the hospitable table, and the hearth of Odysseus.[14] It would be otiose to ask whether the river Styx, by which the gods swear, is a thing or a god. When the invocation in an oath is addressed to a thing, it can be a thing associated intimately with authority, such as the scepter, or a

---

8. For example, *Il.* 10.329; 15.36; 19.258; *Od.* 5.184; 14.158 = 17.155 = 20.230; 19.303. Also in the related procedure of *horkia: Il.* 7.411.

9. *Il.* 14.274. Gods as witnesses (*martyroi*) are also mentioned in the related procedures of *rhētra* (*Od.* 14.393-400) and *horkia* (*Il.* 3.280; 22.255, cf. 262, 266). Though related to *horkos* (oath), as the name indicates, *horkia* is a different procedure, elucidated by D. Cohen, "'Horkia' and 'horkos' in the *Iliad*," *RIDA*, 3d ser., 27 (1980): 49-68. *Horkion, horkia* can be used of the sacrificial victims offered when an oath is sworn: *SIG* 4.9-10; 45.43-44. The meaning of *horkion* in the decree about the settlement at Kyrene (*SEG* 9.3 = Meiggs and Lewis no. 5) might deserve study.

10. *Il.* 1.86; 23.43; *Od.* 20.339.

11. *Il.* 1.234-39.

12. *Il.* 15.36-40.

13. *Od.* 20.339.

14. *Od.* 14.158-59 = 17.155-56 = 20.230-31; at 19.303-4 the table is omitted.

thing regarded with respect by the person swearing, such as the bed of Hera and Zeus, the sufferings of Odysseus, or his hearth. In short, it is a thing of awe.

That observation may have a bearing on the imprecation in Homeric oaths. The imprecation is only stated rarely in the explicit text of the poems. When Agamemnon gains reconciliation with Achilles, he concludes his oath by saying:

> If I have sworn any of these things falsely, may the gods inflict on me very many sufferings, as many as they inflict when someone sins against them in swearing. (*Il.* 19.264-65)

An imprecation should often be understood in Homeric oaths. This follows from a recurrent phrase about gods beneath the earth "who punish people, whenever anyone swears a false oath."[15] Should one then suppose that the invocation in oaths takes its meaning from the implied or explicit imprecation, that is, gods are invoked so that they will punish anyone who swears falsely? To assert this as a universal rule would be unduly rationalistic, even though some Homeric oaths contain an expectation that falsehood will incur divine punishment. When the invocation is addressed to a thing, there is no direct implication of supernatural punishment. When Achilles swears by the scepter, when Telemachos invokes the sufferings of his father, and when others invoke the hearth of Odysseus, there is no simple implication that the thing invoked will bring about punishment for falsehood. Rather the person swearing associates his assertion with a thing of awe. The same consideration explains the gestures mentioned occasionally in connection with oaths. When Hera promised Pasithea to Hypnos, she put one hand on the earth and one on the sea. Menelaos bade Antilochos swear standing in front of his horses and his chariot, holding his whip in his hands, and touching his horses. Thus the person invited to swear was to associate his words with things he held in respect.

In content Homeric oaths are of two kinds. They refer either to the future or to the past. That is, they may say that something will be done in future or they may assert a putative matter of past fact. Oaths referring to the future are frequent and can be subdivided into two kinds, promises and prophecies. In a promissory oath the person swearing says that he

---

15. *Il.* 3.279; 19.260.

will do something; oaths of this kind are frequent.¹⁶ In a prophetic oath the person swearing says that someone else will do something. When such an oath is sworn by a powerful person, its force is much the same as that of a promissory oath. When Achilles swears that no harm shall come to Kalchas as long as Achilles is alive, his utterance differs in grammar from a promise but not in meaning.¹⁷ Oaths that are purely prophetic are sworn by people who believe that they know what will happen. Such oaths cluster in the later part of the *Odyssey,* as the time approaches for the vengeance of Odysseus.¹⁸

Toward understanding the oath tendered by Menelaos to Antilochos, oaths asserting putative matters of past fact are especially informative, although they are not frequent. They are often purgatorial, that is, the person swearing denies that he has done something. Two such oaths call for attention here. When Zeus woke up on Mount Ida and saw that Poseidon was fighting for the Achaians, he suspected that Hera had tricked him. He scolded and threatened her. In reply she swore that it was not through her will that Poseidon had intervened, but he was acting of his own accord (*Il.* 15.36-44). She invoked an impressive list of gods and things of awe, as well she might. For her assertion was false. Yet Zeus did not punish her. He was content with the fear he had inspired in Hera and he told her to send Iris and Apollo to him. The scene on Mount Ida is comical in a grotesque way and therefore does not furnish ground for extensive inference. Yet at least it illustrates the possible falsehood of an oath about the past.

The other oath on a putative fact of the past is sworn by Agamemnon in the course of his reconciliation with Achilles. The tone is of the highest seriousness. Agamemnon is engaged in the procedure of *horkia,* which is marked by the sacrifice of an animal, in this case a boar, and brings about a better relation between two people who have been in conflict. Into the procedure Agamemnon inserts an oath, invoking an awesome series of gods: Zeus, the highest and greatest of the gods, Earth, the

---

16. For example, *Il.* 20.313-17; 21.373-76; 22.119-21; *Od.* 4.253-55; 4.746-49; 5.184-87; 10.342-46; 12.298-304; 14.331-33; 15.435-38; 18.55-59; 19.288-90.

17. *Il.* 1.86-91. Prophetic oaths of promissory force are sworn by Achilles at 1.233-44, by Zeus at 19.108-13 and 19.127-29, and by Hektor at 10.328-32. Hektor in the last passage swears that no one but Dolon shall have the horses of Achilles; by adding that Hektor swore a false oath, the poet plays on the relation between prophetic and promissory aspects.

18. *Od.* 14.151-64; 17.155-59 (this is in form present, not future, but for its reference to the future the next passage may be compared); 19.300-307; 20.227-34.

Sun, and the Erinyes who punish, beneath the earth, anyone who has sworn falsely. Agamemnon asserts that he has not engaged in sexual intercourse with Briseis, the captive whom he had taken from Achilles and is about to restore.[19] Perhaps a reader may wonder whether this assertion is true. Ultimately no meaning can be attached to a question about the truth or falsehood of an assertion on a matter of factual detail in a work of fiction. But the question prompts two observations. One is that in the course of the reconciliation Achilles neither acknowledges nor doubts the truth of Agamemnon's assertion. The other is that the poet has not said whether the assertion is true.

The two oaths, sworn by Hera and Agamemnon, have a feature in common. Each is uttered to appease another person, whose anger has been aroused and who is now in the stronger position. In that situation an assertion sworn by the inferior person on a putative matter of past fact can be of value to the person in the stronger position, even if the assertion is false. A person who swears to a falsehood on a matter of past fact invites punishment at the hands of the gods. Supernatural vengeance is not mechanical in Greek thought. It comes about in unexpected ways, a matter that fascinated Herodotos and the tragedians. If Agamemnon uttered a falsehood on oath as he prepared to restore Briseis to Achilles, he could not foresee precisely how he would suffer in consequence at the hands of the gods. He could not be strictly sure that he would suffer at all. But he could know that he was likely to suffer. If he swore a falsehood, his condition became in consequence precarious. Therefore he would have more need of the alliance of Achilles. That is why Achilles, who understood the diplomacy of Homeric oaths, did not ask about the truth or falsehood of Agamemnon's assertion. Homer composed for audiences who understood the same diplomacy. They appreciated the ambiguity consequent on Agamemnon's oath and could recognize that each arm of the ambiguity brought benefit to Achilles. If Agamemnon's assertion was true, Achilles recovered a captive who had not been touched by the other man. If the assertion was false, Achilles gained superiority over Agamemnon, since the latter would have even greater need of his loyalty.

Dikē as a Mode of Proof

The audiences who listened to the *Iliad* at the Greater Panathenaia understood the force of the word "(not) voluntarily" and the nature of

---

19. *Il.* 19.258-65; cf. 175-77, 191. On the procedure see Cohen, n. 9 above.

Homeric oaths, when they heard the account of the dispute between Menelaos and Antilochos. After saying that he would provide a *dikē,* Menelaos invited Antilochos to swear in terms that Menelaos had formulated. The crucial word in the formulation was *hekōn* ("voluntarily"). If Antilochos swore the oath as tendered to him, he would divorce himself from the deed he had committed in driving his chariot ahead into the narrow part of the course. Since Antilochos had performed that deed, he could scarcely swear the oath without asserting a falsehood. If he swore a falsehood, he would invite the vengeance of the gods and perhaps of men too, for disputes among the Homeric Achaians could easily get out of control as in the first book of the *Iliad*. In some circumstances a party might swear an apparent falsehood and the other party might acquiesce in this for the sake of advantages accruing to him, but the circumstances of the dispute between Antilochos and Menelaos were not of this kind.

Three conclusions are to be drawn from the outcome of that dispute.

1. A *dikē* is not a judgment. The *dikē* uttered by Menelaos was not an assertion that the mare belonged to him or that it belonged to Antilochos. It was not a settlement of the dispute but a proposed mode of bringing the dispute to a settlement without violence. To use a convenient term, the *dikē* was a mode of proof ("Beweisverfahren," Thür, n. 1, above). But the word *proof* must not be allowed to import any modern expectation of demonstrating a matter of fact to the satisfaction of a disinterested judge. No judge takes part in settling the dispute between Menelaos and Antilochos; bystanders are present but they are passive. The *dikē* provided by Menelaos serves as a mode of proof because Antilochos yields to the challenge.
2. A *dikē,* a mode of proof, can be the formulation of an oath that one party is invited to swear. This does not exclude the possibility that other modes of proof were known to Homeric thought.
3. Formulation of the proposed oath can be a delicate matter. By inserting the words "by a trick" into his formulation, Menelaos prejudged the question, whether the deed of Antilochos had been in itself a wrongful deed. He left Antilochos a choice between divorcing himself from the deed by swearing a relatively patent falsehood and declining to swear. In yielding Antilochos mentioned his youth. As the younger man he had lower standing in the community. If the parties to a dispute were more nearly equal, it might

be more difficult to formulate an oath in such terms that they would desist from their dispute without bloodshed.

Dikē as a mode of bringing a dispute to an end without violence is recognized in the *Works and Days* of Hesiod. He says:[20]

> The son of Kronos has laid down this law for men, that it is for fish and animals and flying birds to eat one another, since there is no *dikē* among them. But to men he has given *dikē,* which proves to be by far the best.

An utterance of a modern jurist deserves to be compared with these words:

> Law for our purposes may reasonably be regarded as the means adopted to institutionalize dispute situations and to validate decisions given in the process whose specific object is to inhibit further unregulated conflict. (A. Watson, *The Evolution of Law,* 69)

The language chosen by Professor Watson is less rhythmical than that of Hesiod, but both say the same thing. Both recognize that the goal of *dikē* or of law is to resolve disputes without violence. They agree also in what they omit. Neither of them says that the administration of justice must ascertain the truth about the facts leading to the dispute. Perhaps sometimes ascertaining factual truth may help toward resolving a dispute, but it is no necessary part of *dikē*. A procedure qualifies as *dikē,* or as law in the most rudimentary sense, provided that it brings about a solution without bloodshed. Again, neither Hesiod nor Watson insists that the dispute must be resolved by application of an acknowledged law, or to put the matter another way, that the solution reached must be just. Perhaps sometimes a dispute can be resolved more readily if a rule acknowledged to be just is applied. But the function of *dikē* at its basic level is not the exalted one of applying an ideal rule. The essential function of *dikē* is the humbler one of resolving a dispute without violence. Hesiod and later authorities are right in endorsing *dikē*. It is usually better for men to go to law than to eat one another.

---

20. 276–80. In *Athenian Republic* (University Park: Pennsylvania State University Press, 1987), 82, I thought that Hesiod portrayed an authoritarian way of administering justice. I was wrong.

There is more to be discerned in the *Works and Days* of Hesiod, but before that is noted, attention should be given to modes of proof in other contexts: Homeric, Mesopotamian, and Germanic. Apart from the quarrel between Menelaos and Antilochos, the *Iliad* presents another scene where peaceful resolution of a dispute is attempted. When Hephaistos made a new shield for Achilles, he engraved on it many designs. One of them showed a city at peace, where a dispute was in progress (18.497-508). The elders sat on polished stones in a sacred circle. They held scepters in their hands and each of them offered his *dikē* in turn. A prize of two talents of gold was to be given to the one among them who offered a *dikē* in the most straight fashion. The people stood around shouting for each side. The dispute concerned the payment (*poinē,* wergild) to be made because a man had been killed. The two disputants had come to seek a *peirar* from a wise man (*histōr*). By the "wise man" one should understand the elders or the one among them who offered the most straight *dikē*. The word *peirar* meant originally "a rope," hence "a measuring rope"; consequently it could be used of a limit or of fair distribution. The *peirar* desired by the two men will be provided in the most straight *dikē*.

The pleas of the two parties used to be a philologist's crux. A recent inquiry offers a solution that surmounts the recognized difficulties, and there does not seem to be occasion for improving on it.[21] On this view the lines stating the pleas mean:

> The one asserted that he had paid in full and demonstrated this to the multitude, but the other refused to accept anything.

That is, the one party made an assertion about the past, but the other uttered a refusal directed to the present and future. The former, the man who had killed the victim, said that he had already paid the wergild in full. Evidently some of the victim's relatives had accepted the payment. But one of the relatives, the party in the dispute portrayed on the shield,

---

21. M. Gagarin, *Drakon and Early Athenian Homicide Law* (New Haven: Yale University Press, 1981), 13-16; cf. Sealey, *Athenian Republic,* 78-80. Earlier discussions include W. Leaf, *The Iliad,* 2d. ed. (London: Macmillan, 1902), 2:610-14; H.H. Pflüger, "Die Gerichtsszene auf dem Schilde des Achilleus," *Hermes* 77 (1942): 140-48; H.J. Wolff, "The Origin of Judicial Litigation among the Greeks," *Traditio* 4 (1946): 34-49; P. Chantraine, *Grammaire homérique,* 2 Syntaxe (Paris: Klincksieck, 1953), 335 n. 1. They had reached an impasse.

was recalcitrant. He neither admitted nor denied the truth of the killer's assertion, that he had paid. He disregarded it. He refused to accept any payment and so he retained his right of retaliation.

The parties were arguing at cross-purposes. The recalcitrant relative of the victim did not address himself to what the killer said but raised a different issue. In jurist's language, the issue had not been joined. The elders were not presented with a question of fact, such as might receive an affirmative or negative answer in the light of evidence. They were presented with a tangled dispute. Ingenuity would be required to bring the dispute a step nearer to solution. In addition the elders had to recognize the risk of violence. The people stood around shouting for one side or the other. In other words each of the disputants commanded a political following in the community.

In the context of this scene it is easy to suppose that the *dikē* expected of the elders was a mode of proof, such as an oath to be tendered to one of the parties. Each elder would decide which of the parties he should invite to swear. The elder would have to choose the words for formulating the oath, and he would probably include words that had power in carrying a dispute forward toward a solution; an oath tendered to the killer might, for example, include the word "not voluntarily." In offering his *dikē* each successive elder, except the first, could take into account the response of the crowd to the proposals of his predecessors. The parties to the dispute on the shield were evidently more or less equal in power, since some bystanders shouted for each; at least neither of them was so inferior as to put himself at the mercy of the other and settle out of court. If the *dikē* desired of each elder was a mode of proof such as an oath, a straight *dikē* would be a formulation that both parties and their adherents were willing to accept, since both recognized that it balanced their rights evenly; it drew a straight line of demarcation between them. A *dikē* that favored one party over the other would be crooked.

Because of the difficulty of devising an acceptable mode of proof, it was reasonable to offer the successful elder a large reward.[22] So the

---

22. This answers one of the objections raised by M. Gagarin (*Early Greek Law* [Berkeley: University of California Press, 1986], 29) against the view proposed by Thür and followed here. Gagarin also objects: "The idea of leaving a decision in a dispute between mortals in the hands of an irrational, automatic, divinely determined procedure is completely absent from the poems and seems to violate the basically humanistic spirit of all Greek thought from Homer on." But on the view defended here the procedure was not

Homeric lines describing the dispute yield good sense, if the *dikē* desired was a mode of proof. It must be admitted that those lines do not themselves exclude the alternative interpretation, that the *dikē* desired of the elders was a final judgment. Against this interpretation two considerations can be urged. One is that in the dispute between Menelaos and Antilochos the *dikē* was a mode of proof (by oath), and the word *dikē* ought to have the same significance in the dispute on the shield of Achilles. The other objection arises from classical Athenian procedure. This was characterized by two stages. The parties presented themselves first before an archon (for *anakrisis*) and then before a court of judges (*dikastai*). Likewise in the Homeric disputes there are two stages, first the propounding of a mode of proof and then its execution by a party (if, for example, he swears a tendered oath or refuses to swear). As will be shown later (chap. 5), it is not difficult to discern a line of historical development from the one type of procedure to the other. The function of the Athenian archon developed from the task performed by the Homeric elder, and a new mode of proof, in which each party swore to the truth of his claim, replaced the formulation of an oath tendered to one party. But before pursuing that line of development it will be proper to look at other societies, where relatively similar modes of proof are attested, and to ask how among Greeks resolution of disputes by judicial litigation came to be compulsory.

Modes of Proof in Mesopotamian and Germanic Law

Mesopotamian court procedure of the Neo-Sumerian and Old Babylonian periods will require discussion in a later chapter. Here it suffices to note the outcome of trials. The judgment concluding proceedings in court could be definitive or conditional. A definitive judgment was a finding by the judges for the plaintiff or the defendant. A conditional judgment was the formulation by the judges of an oath that one of the parties was invited to swear. The proposed oath was an assertion about a putative matter of fact in the past. After the judges had thus rendered a conditional judgment, the participants went to a temple, since an oath

---

divinely determined; it was nothing but a way of bringing a dispute to an end without bloodshed. The use made of the loaded word "(ir)rational" is unfortunate; people consider procedures rational if they are accustomed to them. On the other hand Gagarin is surely right against Thür in believing that the issue was not "a simple matter of fact, whether or not the *poinē* has been paid."

asserting a matter of past fact, unlike a promissory oath that made an undertaking for the future, could only be sworn in a temple. If the party to whom the oath was tendered refused to swear, he lost his case and could only hope at best to reach a settlement with his adversary out of court.[23] The similarity to Homeric procedure might provoke any of several comments, but each would be too speculative to be pursued with profit.

Early Germanic law is more complex and more informative. Two modes of proof from the pre-Christian period call for note. First there was proof by oath. In the simplest form of this procedure the oath was formulated by one party and the other was invited to swear. The wording was formulaic. The party swearing the oath guaranteed the truth of his assertion by offering to surrender valuables, as in the *legis actio sacramento* at Rome. Invocation of a god was not essential to this procedure; a god was only invoked in cases where seizure of the valuables in the event of a falsehood was foreseen as to be carried out by the god. In content the oath referred to the past; in form it was often an oath of denial (a purgatorial oath).

The other mode of proof has no certain parallel in Greek practice. It was trial by battle. Each party had a second with him. The place for the duel was measured beforehand, and if either party stepped outside the measured boundaries, he lost his case because he had fled. In both modes of proof the aim was to induce one party to yield, not to ascertain factual truth in a manner that could convince a disinterested person.[24] Later, after the acceptance of Christianity, trial by ordeal was introduced (although it was opposed by the church from the ninth century onward). This presupposed a God who knew the truth and upheld it. The pagan gods were not omniscient and not always veracious.[25]

Possibly a recollection of trial by battle may be discerned in the third book of the *Iliad*. There a duel is arranged between Menelaos and Paris

---

23. A. Walther, *Das altbabylonische Gerichtswesen* (Leipzig: Hinrichs, 1917), 191–95, 212–18; J.G. Lautner, *Die richterliche Entscheidung und die Streitbeendigung im altbabylonischen Prozessrechte* (Leipzig: Weicher, 1922), 25–48; A. Falkenstein, *Die neusumerischen Gerichtsurkunden* (Munich: Bayerische Akademie der Wissenschaften, 1956), 1:62–79.

24. Amira and Eckhardt, *Germanisches Recht*, 2:166–74.

25. Ibid., 2:174–77. Gagarin (*Early Greek Law*, 29–30, and "The Nature of Proofs in Antiphon," *CP* 85 [1990]: 22–32, at 26–29) says mistakenly that all the early Germanic procedures "were crucially dependent on the general belief in, or at least acceptance of, an almighty divinity, whose hand would guide the procedure to a just outcome" (*CP*, 29).

in the hope that this may determine the outcome of the war. What the poet describes is a fight, not a mode of proof; there is no ritual challenge or shaking of hands, such as characterize the Germanic procedure. But during the preparations for the fight Hektor and Odysseus "first measured out a place" (3.315). Apparently the poet knew of a ritual procedure in which the place for the fight was measured out, as in Germanic trial by battle.

Compulsory Litigation

So far this chapter has traced underlying ideas (principles, concepts, and aims) about resolving disputes. An aim of bringing a dispute to an end has been recognized. So has a concept of procedure as a conflict (Greek *agōn,* Old High German *strît,* Middle High German *krieg*), in which one party will be induced to yield. Attention has still to be given to a principle that forbids recourse to violence. Such a principle is assumed, for example, by Hesiod in the *Works and Days*. The occasion or professed occasion of the poem is a dispute between Hesiod and his brother, Perses, over the property inherited from their father. The antecedents of the poem are not wholly clear; it seems that the brothers had divided the estate and a lawsuit had taken place, but Perses was dissatisfied and threatened to go to law again.[26] Hesiod composed the poem to dissuade Perses from doing so. He envisaged only two alternatives, litigation and a settlement by agreement out of court.

But let it be supposed again that two men have a dispute and there is no court. Possibly, by one of the modes of proof discussed above, they will reach a settlement without violence. They may be helped toward this by further persons, who may or may not be disinterested, benevolent, or honest. If one or both of the parties is not sure of his physical strength or of his political influence in the community, he may have a motive for seeking a peaceful settlement. But alternatively it may happen that none of the factors inhibiting violence is effective. Then the aggrieved party will perhaps take the thing in dispute by force, or he may take things of equal or greater value from his adversary, or he may impose physical restraints on the adversary to make him pay up. The general word for such activities is *self-help.* As long as there is no authority that compels

---

26. Hes. *Works* 27–41, 394–97; for discussion see M. Gagarin, "Hesiod's Dispute with Perses," *TAPhA* 104 (1974): 103–11.

recourse to court, an aggrieved person is entitled to engage in self-help. There is no principle of the talion that limits recovery to the amount of the loss, and an act of self-help can in turn provoke a feud.

The question must accordingly be faced, how did compulsory litigation (the authoritative requirement of recourse to a court) replace self-help in Greece? The words "in Greece" must be included in the question because, to anticipate, there is good reason to believe that the development was different in different places. The question is not merely an antiquarian question about origins. For although the question alludes to the obscurity of a preliterate or scarcely literate age, it subsumes within itself a question about Greeks of the classical period: what reason could they give for their insistence that disputes be brought to court? This in turn is part of the larger question, how did Greeks of the fully literate period conceive their judicial institutions?

Two answers have been offered lately to the question of the origin of judicial litigation in Greece. The one answer supposes that the starting point was voluntary recourse to arbitration. At first, it is suggested, the parties to a dispute sometimes sought out a third person of their own accord and invited him to arbitrate. Later public opinion encouraged such recourse with growing intensity. Finally the practice became compulsory. In favor of this theory it is urged that early Greek literature told many stories of people who quarreled but had recourse to arbitration.[27] But, in any age, disputants may invoke arbitration if they are well behaved or afraid of the consequences of being stubborn. The problem is to explain how compulsion came to be imposed even on people who did not shrink from being stubborn. The theory that would derive compulsory litigation from voluntary arbitration fails for several reasons. It does not explain how the mere force of public opinion could make an aggrieved person abandon his right of self-help. If, however, that was achieved, the theory does not explain how there came to be a further role for public authority to exercise, after public opinion had supposedly achieved the desired goal. Moreover, the theory does not explain the survival of features of self-help in classical Athenian procedure. The surviving features were not mere relics but material steps. For example, if a court found for the plaintiff, the latter had the burden

---

27. Gagarin, *Early Greek Law,* 19–50; Gagarin observes that the scenes of arbitration are formal and public, and he concludes: "the evidence for the voluntary submission of disputes is overwhelming" (44).

of executing the judgment; that is, he set about completing an act of self-help from which he had been held back during the trial.[28]

The other theory, propounded by the late H.J. Wolff (n. 28), reconstructs a typical occurrence on the following lines. Let it be supposed that a dispute has arisen; the one party, the plaintiff in modern terms, believes that his right has been infringed—in whatever way—by the other. In a situation where there is no court the plaintiff begins an act of self-help by setting off in pursuit of his adversary. But the defendant flees to a public officer—of whatever kind—and asks for protection. The officer extends temporary protection to the defendant and calls a court—of whatever kind—into session to judge the issue. If the outcome of proceedings before the court is a finding for the plaintiff, he is authorized to resume his act of self-help, which had been interrupted for the duration of the trial; the public officer withdraws protection. If on the other hand the finding is for the defendant, public authority, which may still be rudimentary, does what it can to help him.

This theory explains how recourse to a court could become compulsory; the public officer inhibits the plaintiff's act of self-help. As Wolff said, "judicial litigation came about . . . through the substitution of controlled self-help for uncontrolled self-help" (n. 28 above, 82). The theory explains many features of self-help that continued in classical procedure. The plaintiff, for example, was called "he who pursues" (*ho diōkōn*), and the defendant was called "he who flees" (*ho pheugōn*). The theory explains why each Athenian trial proceeded in two stages. It began with a preliminary hearing, called *anakrisis,* before a public officer, typically one of the nine archons. This was followed by a definitive trial before a *dikastērion*. Although *anakrisis* may have served an additional purpose, to be noted later, it reflects at least the initial step where a person suffering pursuit sought the protection of a public officer. The theory allows for the modest extent of public authority in early Greece. The person spoken of as a public officer could perhaps better be recognized as a private person performing a public task; that possibility will receive attention

---

28. The objections were stated by Wolff, "The Origin of Judicial Litigation," 31-34. Gagarin (*Early Greek Law,* 27-28) maintains against Wolff that in the scene on the shield of Achilles the parties submit their dispute to the elders voluntarily. That interpretation is tenable. But Gagarin has not met Wolff's objections to deriving judicial litigation from arbitration. The plaintiff's burden of executing the judgment is illustrated by the predicament of Demosthenes after he had won his case against Aphobos; see Dem. 30 and 31 passim.

in the next chapter. The theory acknowledges that at an early stage public authority could not do much for a successful defendant. If an Athenian was accused of homicide and argued that he had not intended to kill, and if the court upheld him, he was told to leave Attica by a stated route within a stated number of days; that is, he was given a safe-conduct to the border.[29] The state was not strong enough to protect him against vengeful relatives of the dead man permanently, but it gave him a chance to escape into exile.

The weak character of public authority is reflected also in the condition of the successful plaintiff. He had the burden of executing the judgment; that is, he resumed his act of self-help. If in executing the judgment he tried to seize property and was impeded, classical Athens could do no more than offer him the "action against being kept out" (*dikē exoulēs*). If he won this action, the person impeding him was ordered to pay twice the value that had been at issue.[30]

Further features of classical Athenian procedure provide support for Wolff's theory. A good illustration is the "action alleging wrongful arrest as an adulterer" (*graphē adikōs heirchthēnai hōs moichon*). If an Athenian discovered an adulterer with his wife, he was allowed to kill the adulterer.[31] But the Athenians recognized that this right might be abused. So they did not deny the right of self-help but they imposed restrictions; the aggrieved husband must take the adulterer in the act of adultery and must have witnesses.[32] These conditions were difficult to fulfill. A characteristically Athenian solution was devised. If an Athenian found a man in his house and suspected him of adultery, the householder could tie up the suspect; thus he began an act of self-help. But consequently the suspect could not flee to a public officer and ask for protection. Instead, any Athenian could initiate the action alleging wrongful arrest as an adulterer. The effect of opening the action was to bring the husband and the suspect into court. There each of them tried to convince the *dikastai*. If the court found for the husband, he was allowed in open court to do to the adulterer anything short of touching him with a knife.[33]

---

29. Dem. 23.72; Ruschenbusch, "*Phonos*," Historia 9 (1960): 139.
30. Solon F 36; cf. n. 28 above on the predicament of Demosthenes.
31. Dem. 23.53; cf. Ar. *AP.* 57.3.
32. Solon F 28c; Lys. 1 passim.
33. [Dem.] 59.66; the action has been elucidated by E. Ruschenbusch, "Der Ursprung des gerichtlichen Rechtsstreits bei den Griechen," *Symposion 1977* (Cologne: Böhlau, 1982), 1–8 at 5–6. The *graphe moicheias* (Ar. *AP.* 59.3) may be an abbreviated name for the same action.

Wolff tried to ground his reconstruction in the judicial scene portrayed on the shield of Achilles (*Il.* 18.497–508). In the two pleas translated above (p. 103), it is noteworthy that the poet presents first the defendant, who asserts that he has paid in full. After that the poet adds that the other party, the plaintiff, refused to accept anything. The order in which the poet reports the pleas should be understood as the order in which he imagined them to be uttered. That is, the poet supposed that in court the defendant speaks first. This order contradicts modern expectations but it conforms to Wolff's hypothesis; the defendant has to give a reason why public authority should protect him against an aggrieved person's act of self-help. Except in this one significant detail the scene lends little support to Wolff's view. In particular the Homeric description does not show who extends protection to the defendant. One cannot even be sure whether the occurrence is arbitration or a trial. The eagerness of both parties to get a *peirar* from a "wise man" (l. 501) suggests voluntary recourse to arbitration, but the solemn character of the scene, especially the scepters held by the elders as symbols of authority, may indicate power to compel attendance. The Homeric scene is not likely to lend much support to any theory. The poet has portrayed a single moment of the proceedings; he had no reason to trace their further development or say what outcome was reached in the dispute.

Wolff's theory is of value not merely because it offers an explanation of origins but even more because it elucidates classical Athenian procedure. In doing so it discovers an underlying principle. Classical Athens, like modern societies, restrained an aggrieved person from engaging in self-help, but the reasons for the restraint differ. In modern belief, self-help is an abomination, to be avoided at all costs. This belief springs from the ambitions of mediaeval kings, who asserted their right to preserve the peace. The belief has been inherited and extended through the even greater ambitions of the legal profession, which seeks to assert its power over society (cf. chap. 2, p. 42). The Athenians held a different belief. They recognized that self-help was legitimate, but they saw that it could get out of hand. So they imposed restrictions on the exercise of the acknowledged right. The development was from uncontrolled self-help to controlled self-help.

CHAPTER 5

How to Resolve Disputes II: Athens

This essay is a quest for the original spring of Greek justice, and the last chapter inquired into the earliest methods employed by Greeks for resolving disputes, so far as those methods were recollected in Greek writings and reflected as relics in the mature practice of the Athenians. The chapter espoused a theory that explains how an action at law could arise in Greek conditions. The theory assumed the existence of a public officer, but his nature was not specified. So there is unfinished business for this chapter to attend to. It will inquire into the public officer of the emergent Greek city. Public officers played a part in forensic procedure at Athens in all periods. So the chapter will treat in outline the Athenian law of actions. In doing so it will try to answer the question, whether the Athenians developed a concept of crime.

Basileis and Archontes

Until recently many people believed in a story of early Greek development that ran on the following lines.[1] It was supposed that extensive migrations followed the collapse of the civilizations of the late Bronze Age. Each host on the march had a single leader; for wherever there were two leaders, there were two hosts. The leader alone took decisions, but he sought the advice of influential men in his following beforehand, and if he disregarded their advice persistently, he was likely to be overthrown. When he had taken his decision, he announced it to a parade of the warriors; in this way he gave them their orders for action. After a migrating host had conquered land and settled on it, a hereditary monarchy

---

1. *Mea quoque culpa: A History of the Greek City-States ca. 700–338 B.C.* (Berkeley: University of California Press, 1976), 23–24.

developed from the military leader and retained command in warfare as its most authoritarian function. The king's advisers, men of influence in the community, became institutionalized as a council, and the parade of all who could bear arms continued as a political assembly. But monarchy was more vulnerable in personnel than a council. When the king died, his heir might be a minor, or the succession might be disputed. The council on the other hand was immortal. So as time passed, kings were replaced with annual officers, who associated with the council. Thus aristocracy replaced monarchy, and Greek cities were launched on a path of constitutional development that led to varied results.

In recent years this reconstruction has been challenged successfully and replaced by a more plausible pattern. Archaeological evidence for the supposedly powerful kings of the Geometric Age is lacking; no traces have been found of palaces or of royal tombs. Kings are likewise absent from early lyric poetry. *Basilēes* are plentiful in the Homeric and Hesiodic poems, too plentiful to be monarchs. There are many of them in a single community, thirteen for example in Phaiakia. Hesiod in the *Works and Days* habitually speaks of *basilēes* in the plural within the single community to which he and his brother belong. Evidently the *basilēes* of Hesiod and Homer were leading men of the community but nothing more. In the *Iliad* the supreme commander of the Achaians has the title of *anax,* perhaps a reminiscence of the Bronze Age. It does not figure among the public institutions of historic Greece (except in Cyprus, where it has a non-Homeric meaning, being used in the plural of the ruler's sons). In the classical period powerful men, including Macedonian kings, gave themselves lines of descent reaching back to the heroic past, but these were fictitious. So was the list of Athenian kings; it was constructed by Hellanikos. Royal genealogies for several cities, especially of Ionia, are preserved by late writers, notably Pausanias; at best they reflect the imaginative pride of classical families. Many important cities, such as Eretria and Chalkis, did not even have a tradition of kings. For Hesiod (*Works* 654-55), Amphidamas of Chalkis was Amphidamas of Chalkis; he is first called *basileus* in the *Contest of Homer and Hesiod,* a work probably not composed before 400 B.C.[2]

The newer theory traces development, not from monarchy to aristoc-

---

2. The material of this paragraph is taken from R. Drews, *Basileus: The Evidence for Kingship in Geometric Greece* (New Haven: Yale University Press, 1983). That of the next is mostly from M. Stahl, *Aristokraten und Tyrannen im archaischen Athen* (Stuttgart: Steiner, 1987), 137-232, especially 150-75; on prestate conditions see 140-44.

racy within a public framework, but from prestate conditions to the beginnings of public institutions. At the starting point in the Geometric period there was no public framework, no organized state or *polis*. People lived in villages that were collections of households lacking civic organization. For some villages, natural features, such as mountains and seas, provided boundaries. Status and wealth varied much within each village. The centers of power were strong households. Authority was domestic, not public. But sometimes there were public tasks to be performed—a cult to be conducted, for example, or a war to be fought against the next village, or a dispute between two men to be brought to a peaceful outcome, if possible. These tasks were public, for they bore on the welfare of the whole village. But there were no public officers to perform them. Instead they were carried out by men from powerful households, such men serving temporarily as priests, commanders in warfare, or judicial magistrates. Hesiod's *basilēes* were private persons performing public tasks in virtue of their standing in the community.

From the eighth century onward there was some growth of prosperity and population; in some places it can be recognized from the spread of settlement and in some from traces of the first public buildings.[3] So there came a time when *basilēes* of the older type were replaced by elective officials. Usually they served for a year at a time. From the start they may well have been chosen not as single officers but in small numbers; collegiality was a consequence of the jealousy that accompanied Greek ambition. The titles favored for such officers included *basileus* and *archōn*. While public tasks thus generated public officers, gatherings of influential men and of the general community became somewhat regular and formal; a council and an assembly emerged and became distinguished.

Prestate conditions are illustrated in parts of the *Iliad* and the *Odyssey*. In the judicial scene on the shield of Achilles the men who propound modes of proof are called "elders." They do not hold an office. They are private men who are respected and who therefore undertake the public task of bringing a disruptive dispute to a peaceful end. At Ithaka the islanders are not called together until the twentieth year after the departure of Odysseus (*Od.* 2.26-27). There are no public organs functioning of their own momentum on the island. There are several men

---

3. A.M. Snodgrass, *Archaeology and the Rise of the Greek State* (Inaugural lecture, Cambridge: Cambridge University Press, 1977); cf. C.G. Starr: *The Economic and Social Growth of Early Greece, 800-500 B.C.* (Oxford: Oxford University Press, 1977) passim.

of power, each controlling his own house, land, and dependents; one of them has been stronger than the others, until he left for Troy. Geese feed at a trough within his house, and there is a heap of manure near the main entrance, for he is a wealthy farmer.[4] Audiences at the Greater Panathenaia understood the conditions assumed in the poems without the help of a commentary. Indeed even after the work of Solon the public framework of the Athenian state was precarious.[5] It yielded to the private power of Peisistratos.

Homicide

Wolff's theory, presented in the later part of the previous chapter, explains how compulsory recourse to court could come about. A public officer checked the plaintiff's incipient act of self-help by extending protection to the defendant and called a court into session, so that the parties had to present their cases to it. It will be maintained here that this development came about in Athens while there were still no public officers and public tasks were performed by private persons. The argument rests on a feature in the laws of homicide. These require attention now.

For several reasons it is likely that disputes arising from homicide were the earliest material for which the Athenians instituted compulsory litigation. The decree of Teisamenos in 403/2 B.C. required the Athenians to observe the laws of Solon and of Drakon but used different words for them. It called the laws of Solon *nomoi,* the contemporary word for statutes, but it referred to the laws of Drakon by the archaic word, *thesmoi.*[6] Aristotle believed that Drakon had been at work earlier than Solon, although he did not say what the interval was.[7] The judges in most of the courts for homicide were called *ephetai,* whereas those in courts handling other material were called *hēliastai* or *dikastai.* Some historians have thought that *dikastai* of normal type eventually replaced

---

4. *Od.* 17.297–99 (the manure); 19.552–53 (the geese); cf. A.G. Geddes, "Who's who in Homeric society?" *CQ,* n.s., 34 (1984): 17–36. The floor of the house is probably of beaten earth, for men clean it by scraping it with shovels: *Od.* 22.454–56.

5. Cf. the observation of J. Martin, "Die Staatlichkeit Athens blieb trotz der solonischen Reformen prekär" ("Von Kleisthenes zu Ephialtes," *Chiron* 4 [1974]: 5–42, at 12).

6. Andok. 1.83; cf. chapter 2.

7. Ar. *AP.* 4.1; 5.1–2. On possible implications of Aristotle's silence see R. Sealey, "Zum Datum der solonischen Gesetzgebung," *Historia* 28 (1979): 238–41.

ephetai in the ephetic courts.[8] Even so, the name *ephetai* was kept, and it may reflect the earlier origin of the courts for homicide.

Extant information on the Athenian laws of homicide is relatively good. Demosthenes quotes and discusses many of them in the speech *Against Aristokrates* (23.22-99). Before A.D. 1867 the authenticity of the putative laws preserved in the manuscripts of this speech was often doubted; the wording of the laws was strange, and it had been noticed that some putative documents in other speeches of the same orator (especially in speech 18, *On the crown*) were spurious. But in 1867 an inscription of 409/8 B.C. was published. The preamble ordered the recorders of the laws to inscribe "the law of Drakon about homicide" on stone, and the body of the text was provisions on homicide. Even though much of the inscribed text is illegible, enough was preserved to prove the authenticity of many phrases in the laws quoted in the Demosthenic speech. Apart from particular questions of interpretation, the inscription has immeasurable value in that it provides reason for confidence in the laws presented in the manuscripts of this speech.[9]

The first among the substantive provisions of the inscription assigns tasks to the *basileis* and to the *ephetai*. Readers have noticed that *basileis* is plural. In classical Athens only one of the nine archons bore the title of *basileus*. Attempts have been made to explain the plural form in the inscription: perhaps the reference is to different *basileis* of successive years, or to the *basileus* sitting jointly with the *phylobasileis,* the headmen of the four hereditary *phylai* into which the Athenians were divided. These explanations are not compelling, and a better one may be suggested in the light of the prestate conditions outlined in the preceding section. Perhaps, when the first law preserved on the inscription was formulated, Athens did not yet have public officials, such as the nine archons including a *basileus*. The law assigned a public task in jurisdiction to a private person or persons. Patently, if a public task—a task bearing on the well-

---

8. G. Smith, "Dicasts in the Ephetic Courts," *CP* 19 (1924): 353-58; challenged by D.M. MacDowell, *Athenian Homicide Law in the Age of the Orators* (Manchester: Manchester University Press, 1963), 52-57, and Harrison, *Law,* 2:40-42; defended by R. Sealey, "The Athenian Courts for Homicide," *CP* 78 (1983): 275-96, at 294-95.

9. E. Drerup, "Über die bei den attischen Rednern eingelegten Urkunden," *Jahrbücher für classische Philologie,* Supplementband 24 (1898): 221-366, at 223-47 and 264-80. The inscription was edited anew with improved readings by R.S. Stroud, *Drakon's Law on Homicide* (Berkeley: University of California Press, 1968). It is available as *IG* I³. 104 = Meiggs and Lewis no. 86.

being of the community, such as settlement of a disruptive dispute—was to be performed by private agency, the agents might be plural. If this explanation is right, it follows that at least this one among the laws inscribed in 409/8 B.C. had originated at an early date.

The inscription has had much discussion, and some uncertainties remain. For the most part its difficulties are not germane to the present inquiry, and so brief treatment will suffice. Starting from the inscription and the Demosthenic speech, a defensible view offers the following reconstruction of the earliest stage in the Athenian law of homicide. The killer, it is suggested, was pursued by the relatives of the victim and sought protection at the hands of one or more powerful men (*basileis*). The latter gave him temporary protection and called a court, the fifty-one *ephetai*, into session to judge the issue. If the *ephetai* found by vote for the plaintiff, the defendant was deprived of public protection. In language cited elsewhere by Demosthenes from the laws on homicide, the unsuccessful defendant was declared *atimos;* that is, anyone could kill him with impunity. But if the *ephetai* found for the defendant, he was given a safe-conduct to the border. There was no public authority to protect him indefinitely, but he could be given a chance to escape into the relative safety of exile. The law recognized the prospect that the killer might negotiate a settlement (*aidesis*) with the relatives of the victim. That practice, a matter of private bargaining, was doubtless older than the earliest attempt to impose explicit regulation, but the finding of the court might strengthen the one party or the other when the level of payment (*poinē*, wergild) was under negotiation.[10]

What calls for note here is the tasks distributed to the *basileis* and the *ephetai* in the first law on the inscription of 409/8 B.C. The law provides that the *basileis* shall *dikazein* and the *ephetai* shall *diagnōnai*.[11] Virtually the same verbs are employed to distinguish the tasks of the officers and the court in another law, which is preserved in the manuscripts of Demosthenes (23.28):

Let the magistrates (*archontes*) introduce cases of the types for which

---

10. This reconstruction owes much to Ruschenbusch, "*Phonos*"; cf. Sealey (n. 8 above) 275-96 and R. Sealey, *Athenian Republic: Democracy or the Rule of Law?* (University Park: Pennsylvania State University Press), 70-77. Demosthenes at 9.44 says that *atimos* occurred in the laws of homicide and explains its force; cf. chap. 1, "*Atimia*." The safe-conduct to the border is indicated by Dem. 23.72.

11. Lines 11-13. Likewise, the task assigned to the *ephetai* is *gnōnai* in line 17 and *diagignōskein* in line 29 (restored from Dem. 23.37-38).

they are severally *dikastai* in response to the citizen who wishes to take action, and let the court (*hēliaia*) *diagignōskein*.

The court to which this law refers is not the *ephetai,* the judges for homicide, but the *heliaia,* the regular court of which the origin was attributed to Solon. The officers mentioned are not the *basileus* or *basileis* but the *archontes,* that is the nine archons in general or perhaps any of the many officers who could bring cases to court in classical Athens. Classical procedure was in two stages. First the parties appeared before an officer, such as one of the nine archons. Each of these had competence for cases of a defined type.[12] The officer conducted a preliminary inquiry (*anakrisis*) and thus brought about joinder of the issue. That is, the inquiry culminated in a question that could be put to a court. At the second stage the two parties appeared before the court and delivered their speeches in turn. The court chose between them by vote of a majority.

In the two laws under consideration the verb *dikazein* specifies the task of the officer (in the language of the orators its meaning was different, as will be noted below). Its meaning can be explained from the Homeric *dikē* recognized in the previous chapter. In the *Iliad* and in the *Works and Days* of Hesiod *dikazein* was to offer a *dikē,* that is, to furnish a mode of proof—for example, to formulate an oath and invite one of the parties to swear it. In the Athenian law of homicide the *basileus* has to *dikazein,* that is, to offer a *dikē,* but the mode of proof he furnishes is of a different kind. His task is to formulate a question that states the issue between the two parties and can be presented to the court for decision. The parties then present their arguments and the *ephetai* decide between them by vote of a majority. In Homeric settlement of disputes one party was challenged to swear an oath. In classical Athenian procedure both parties swore to the truth of their pleas before the officer and then each tried to convince the judges.[13] A rigid and relatively formulaic way of settling disputes was replaced by an argumentative and flexible procedure.

---

12. Aristotle (*AP.* 56–59) reviews the tasks of the nine archons and notes the type of case for which each had competence.

13. E. Ruschenbusch, *Untersuchungen zur Geschichte des athenischen Strafrechts* (Cologne: Böhlau, 1968), 74–77; cf. G. Thür, "Die Todesstrafe im Blutprozess Athens," *Journal of Juristic Papyrology* 20 (1990): 151.

Solonian Procedure

The *ephetai* numbered fifty-one. Provided that every one of them voted, there was sure to be a majority for one side. In classical Athens the standard size of a *dikastērion* was 501, but for some private cases in the fourth century panels of 401 and 201 were employed according to the value of the thing in dispute.[14] Each of the figures is intentionally odd; one has been added to a round figure. The *ephetai,* the oldest court, were doubtless the model for this practice.

In the fourth century Athenian tradition said that Solon had created the *dikastēria.*[15] That was the contemporary word, commonly used by the orators, for the courts. The more conservative language of law preferred the word *hēliaia.* Demosthenes quotes a law on theft, in which the court is called *hēliaia,* but in his explanatory comment he calls it *dikastērion.*[16] Likewise the oath sworn by *dikastai* was called "the oath of the *hēliastai*" or "the *heliastic* oath."[17] Aristophanes refers to *dikastai* with the word *hēliastēs* and the corresponding verb and adjective.[18] In the classical period the role of the public officer in bringing a dispute to a peaceful conclusion had become less weighty than in Homeric procedure. In propounding a mode of proof he no longer challenged one party to swear in terms that the officer formulated. The mode of proof was now argument before a panel of judges, and the officer's task, performed at the *anakrisis,* was to state the issue on which the parties disagreed. The decisive step in achieving the outcome could no longer be the formulation of the mode of proof but was the vote of the judges. So *dikē* came to mean the whole procedure of trial and *dikastai* was used of judges.

Hēliaia, the older word for the court, occurs only in the singular. Evidently a single court sufficed at first, but as judicial business grew, many *dikastēria* came to be needed. Since the words *hēliaia* with its cognates and *dikastērion* with its cognates were interchangeable, the court specified by the one name was the same as that specified by the

---

14. Ar. *AP.* 53.1-3. It is an inexplicable curiosity that in *IG*².1641, lines 25-33, the only epigraphic record giving the number of votes at a trial, the total is 499, with 100 for the plaintiff and 399 for the defendant.

15. Ar. *Pol.* 2.1273b41-1274a2; *AP.* 9.1. These two passages refer to the same event: see Ruschenbusch, *"Hēliaia," Historia* 14 (1965): 383.

16. Dem. 24.105 and 114. The same interchange occurs in Antiph. 6.21 and 23.

17. Dem. 24.148; Hyper. 4.40 (Kenyon).

18. *Knights,* 798; *Wasps,* 195, 772, 891; *Lys.* 380.

other, the only difference being in the number of courts that could sit at the same time. It follows that the archaic *hēliaia* was the same in composition as the classical *dikastērion*. It was a panel of citizens aged at least thirty years and bound by oath; its size may well have been 501, certainly an odd number.[19] Athenian tradition said that Solon had created this court, and this tradition is credible, but its meaning is imprecise.

The quest for the historical Solon has been long and disappointing. The classical Athenians liked to attribute all their laws to him. Some such attributions were tendentious, some perhaps fanciful.[20] Consequently the mere attribution of a law to Solon in extant sources is not sufficient grounds for believing that it was part of his code. Moreover, even if a supposed law of Solon has a good chance of being authentic, one may still be unable to tell what difference it made if the previous condition is not known.[21] This point deserves illustration. The law cited in the fourth century B.C. to regulate bequest and adoption opened thus:

> Concerning those who had not been adopted so as neither to disclaim nor to claim the inheritance, when Solon entered into office, let a man be free to bequeath his property as he wishes, provided that... [several restrictions follow].[22]

The reference to Solon is a reason for accepting the law as authentic. The opening words deny testamentary capacity to men who have been adopted as sons by other men. It follows that adoption was already practised before Solon issued this law. His law did not make an innovation out of nothing; it regulated a practice that was already current.

---

19. Ar. *AP.* 63.3 gives the requirement of age. An old theory said that the *heliaia* was the assembly sitting as a court of appeal. It has been refuted by Ruschenbusch, *"Ephesis," ZSR* 78 (1961): 386-90; idem, *"Heliaia"*; M.H. Hansen, "The Athenian *heliaia* from Solon to Aristotle," *C et M* 33 (1981-82): 9-47; cf. Sealey, *Athenian Republic,* 61-69.

20. Tendentious: Andok. 1.95-96; Dem. 20.89-90. Probably fanciful: Aristoph. *Clouds* 1178-95 (accepted at face value by Plut. *Sol.* 25.4).

21. This difficulty is overlooked by O. Murray, *Early Greece* (Brighton, Sussex: Harvester Press, and Atlantic Highlands, N.J.: Humanities Press, 1980), 189; and by A. Andrewes, *Cambridge Ancient History,* 2d ed., 3.3 (Cambridge, Cambridge University Press, 1982), 389.

22. [Dem.] 46.14; discussed by E. Ruschenbusch, *"Diatithesthai ta heautou:* Ein Beitrag zum sogenannten Testamentsgesetz des Solon," *ZSR* 79 (1962): 307-11; cf. Sealey, *Athenian Republic,* 27.

Since the previous practice is not known and may not have been uniform, one cannot tell what difference Solon's law made.

Considerable parts of Solon's poems are extant. One of them, which appears to be complete, summarizes and defends his public work. Much of it is devoted to his economic reform, the *seisachtheia*. On his other work the poem offers a single sentence:

> I wrote laws (*thesmoi*) alike for the bad man and the good, fitting straight justice (*dikē*) into each.[23]

An argument from silence may be permissible. If Solon had set out to make innovations, surely this poem was the place to say so. His remark suggests that he undertook his task in a more conservative spirit. His aim was to achieve written laws, not novel laws, even though some changes may be unavoidable when customs are reduced to writing. The relation that the quoted sentence sets up between laws (*thesmoi*) and justice (*dikē*) may call to mind the hypothesis drawn in chapter 2 from the casuistic formulation of Athenian laws; issuance of laws in general terms may have sprung from the practice of settling particular disputes.

In chapter 2 the further possibility was noted that some laws had been issued in writing before the work of Solon. Doubtless his compilation was extensive. Probably he tried to provide explicitly for many possible occurrences and expected the *hēliaia* to rule on all other occurrences. This concept of discrete laws with gaps between them remained embedded in Athenian thought and was reflected in the oath of *dikastai*, as has been noted. One cannot tell whether Solon created the *hēliaia* or, finding it already in existence, clarified and extended its competence by legislation.[24] The question has no great importance, if in any case the court of the *ephetai* provided the model for the *hēliaia*.

The work of Solon remains elusive, but an indirect approach to his role in procedural law may be fruitful. From institutional survivals it is

---

23. Solon fr. 36 (West) lines 18–20, from Ar. *AP.* 12.4.

24. The law on theft, quoted at Dem. 24.105, illustrates how legislation might clarify and perhaps extend the competence of the court by specification: "Whenever anyone finds that something is missing, if he recovers it, let the condemnation be in twice the value, but if not, let it be in ten times (?) the value in addition to the payment for responsibility. Let him be bound by the foot in the stocks for five days and five nights, if the heliaia imposes this additional penalty. Let anyone who wishes propose the additional penalty, when the level of penalty is under discussion." The compressed wording, which fails to identify "he" or "him," and the reference to the stocks suggest that the law is old.

possible to reconstruct an early stage in the Athenian law of actions and recognize that stage as in some sense Solonian.[25] Reconstruction can begin from the penalty of *atimia* provided in the laws of homicide (see above, at n. 10). This penalty was negative in character; the community withdrew protection from the unsuccessful defendant and thereby abandoned him to the vengeance of his enemies. A later reform transferred jurisdiction in some cases of homicide from the *ephetai* to the Council of the Areopagos. The reform gave that council competence over the charge of killing an Athenian citizen intentionally with one's own hands. Infliction of the penalty of death on the offender by a public executioner may well have been introduced as part of the same reform. The changes reflect a large growth in public authority. The state had become powerful enough to impose positive penalties, and so Athenians had learned to rely less on private vengeance for protection.[26]

An archaic law of the Athenians provided *atimia* as the penalty for attempting tyranny, a provision that surprised the author of the Aristotelian *Constitution of the Athenians* (16.10). If the early Athenian state could inflict nothing more than the negative penalty of *atimia* for homicide and for attempted tyranny, presumably it could only inflict negative penalties for other misdeeds. Even in classical conditions the successful plaintiff had the burden of executing the judgment in suits for property.

---

25. This reconstruction owes much to Ruschenbusch, *Untersuchungen,* 11–21, 30–47, and idem, "*Dikē kata tinos* und *pros tina,*" ZSR 86 (1969): 386–94.

26. The classical distribution of competence between the Areopagos and the *ephetai* is stated by Ar. *AP.* 57.3–4. The public executioner is known from Dem. 23.69. See Sealey, n. 8 above. Thür ("Die Todesstrafe") offers a different explanation for the introduction of the death penalty, inflicted by public authority, for homicide. He suggests that it was a "side-effect of a greater reform" ("Nebenprodukt einer grösseren Reform," p. 149), and so far I agree. He notes that the accused could withdraw into exile, provided that he did not wait for the conclusion of the trial; if he returned to Attica (without *aidesis*), he could be killed or led away to a public organ for execution (Dem. 23.28). So he suggests that infliction of the death penalty by public authority on the murderer came about when the accused person who stayed was equated with the exiled killer who returned. Against Thür's theory I note that infliction of the death penalty by the state deprived the victim's relatives of their chance to exact payment (*poinē*) from the killer as price for desisting from the feud. Aggrieved relatives would only give up that opportunity when ideas on homicide had changed radically. That change came about, I suggest, when the Athenians learned to look to public authority as their primary source of protection. So infliction of the death penalty by the state was a side effect of a reform that assigned limited competence in homicide to the Areopagos. Thür remarks rightly that the innovation should have evoked discussion (p. 149). On my view discussion of the transfer of limited competence to the Areopagos is reflected in the legends of heroic trials (of Halirrhothios, Kephalos, Orestes) before that Council (cf. Jacoby, *F Gr Hist* III b [Supplement] I, 22–25).

If the court found for the plaintiff, it assessed the value of the thing in dispute and authorized the plaintiff to collect that amount from the defendant. That is, the plaintiff resumed his act of self-help, which had been interrupted for the duration of the trial. He might try to seize property from the defendant. If a third person intervened to impede the seizure, the plaintiff had an action, the *dikē exoulēs,* against the person obstructing him (see chap. 4, at n. 30). Demosthenes had recourse to this action in his dispute with his guardians.

In early Athens the successful plaintiff could follow an alternative course. The Solonian law on bequest, noted above, stated several restrictions; one of them was that a man was not free to bequeath his property if he had been tied up. That is, the law recognized that a man might be lawfully tied up by a private person. The suggested explanation is that a successful plaintiff might seize the person of the defendant in order to make him pay the judgment. If, however, a third person intervened to protect the defendant against personal seizure, the plaintiff had an action against him, "the action for taking away into freedom" (*dikē aphaireseōs eis eleutherian*).[27] The two types of seizure, carried out against property and against the person, resemble somewhat the Roman procedures of *pignoris capio* and *manus iniectio.*

Reconstructed from later Athenian practices, the procedures outlined in the previous three paragraphs probably approximate to the condition emerging from Solon's work, if he was the first to write laws extensively for the Athenians. Some features of this condition may well be older. Seizures in the course of self-help had doubtless been practised long before. The economic reform of Solon, the *seisachtheia,* may have caused a modification, directly or indirectly. In the fourth century people believed that the economic difficulty confronting Solon had arisen because loans had been contracted on the security of the borrower's person; so they held that Solon's remedial measure forbade seizure of the person for failure to repay the loan.[28] The nature of the economic difficulty and

---

27. Ruschenbusch, *Untersuchungen,* 30-40. Likewise the last provision in the first section of the law-code of Gortyn (I, 56 to II, 2) allowed seizure of a person who had been defeated in court.

28. Ar. *AP.* 2.2; 4.5; 6.1; 9.1. This opinion on the character of Solon's work prevailed and was followed by Plutarch (*Sol.* 13.4; 15.2). But it was disputed; Androtion (*F Gr Hist* III B 324 F 34 = Plut. *Sol.* 15.3-4) offered a different hypothesis. Aristotle's account of Solon in *AP.* is argumentative and may be directed against Androtion. Evidently there was no fully decisive evidence available in the fourth century.

therefore the content of Solon's measure are uncertain.[29] But the fourth-century belief shows that a restriction had been placed on seizure of the person, whether by Solon's measure or by interpretation of that measure. The consequence was a distinction between two types of private action, the *dikē pros tina* and the *dikē kata tinos*. In the former, only ownership of specific valuables was at stake; the plaintiff set out to recover something owed to him. The *dikē kata tinos,* on the other hand, had the additional aspect of penalty for delict. It is the older type of action; the plaintiff believed that the defendant had committed a wrong, and so on winning his action the plaintiff had the prospect of exacting a penalty from his adversary. But the Solonian restriction on personal seizure had as a consequence the emergence of the *dikē pros tina,* where only the better right to the valuables was at issue.[30] So now one must ask how penalties were understood in Athenian thought.

Penalties and Actions

This section will review Athenian procedural law in pursuit of the question, whether the Athenians developed a concept of crime, that is, did they treat some injuries to single persons as injuries or threats of injury to the community. Some laws of Solon specified payments for delicts. Rape of a free woman, for example, brought a payment of one hundred drachmas; some insults uttered in specified places incurred a payment of five drachmas; the man who prostituted a woman was to pay twenty drachmas.[31] In the age of Solon public authority was weak, and therefore these sums should not be regarded as positive penalties inflicted by the state. They were ransoms. The defendant who lost his case was abandoned to the plaintiff, who resumed his interrupted act of self-help by seizing the offender, but the law stated the level of ransom by which the wrongdoer could buy himself free. The same development from ransom to delictal payments fixed (or recommended) by law is found in the

---

29. A good hypothesis is propounded by Andrewes (n. 21 above) 377–82; cf. idem, *The Greeks* (London: Hutchinson, 1967), 104–8.

30. Ruschenbusch, "*Dikē kata tinos.*" For a list of *dikai* see J.H. Lipsius, *Attisches Recht und Rechtsverfahren,* 3 vols. (Leipzig: Reisland, 1905-15), 636–773.

31. Plut. *Sol.* 23.1 = F 26; Plut. *Sol.* 21.1 = F 32a; Plut. *Sol.* 23.1 = F 30a. The specified insults in the stated places amounted to incitement to lynch the man calumniated; cf. Ruschenbusch, *Untersuchungen,* 24–27.

Gortynian provisions on sexual offenses; after stating the payments due for adultery with women of varied status, the laws say how the captor is to make an announcement to the relatives of the captive adulterer, bidding them to ransom him within five days (II, 20-36). In the fifth century, as the value of money decreased, new Athenian laws abandoned the system of fixed payments and authorized the courts to assess penalties.[32]

In some private actions (*dikai*) the unsuccessful defendant was required to make two financial payments, one to the plaintiff and one to the state. A person found to have uttered a forbidden insult against a living man in a forbidden place was required to pay three drachmas to the victim and two to the state.[33] In the action against taking movable property by force (*dikē biaiōn*), the unsuccessful defendant was to make equal payments to the plaintiff and to the state.[34] In the *dikē exoulēs* (the action against being kept out, chap. 4, at n. 30), an action that enabled a successful plaintiff to enforce a judgment, the defendant had to pay twice the value of the original judgment; he paid the amount due to the plaintiff and the same amount to the state.[35] The same is true of the other action enabling a plaintiff to execute a judgment, the *dikē aphaireseōs eis eleutherian* (the action for taking away into freedom); the unsuccessful defendant paid equal sums to the plaintiff and to the state.[36] Should it be supposed that the payments made to the state in these actions sprang from a concept of crime, that is, from the belief that the community as well as the victim was harmed or threatened by the misdeed?

A better explanation can be offered on the basis of Wolff's theory

---

32. Ruschenbusch, *Untersuchungen,* 11-15; cf. H.J. Wolff, "The *Dikē Blabēs* in Demosthenes, *Or.,* LV," *AJP* 64 (1943): 316-24. For an illustration of the change to *aestimatio poenae* see E. Ruschenbusch, "*Hybreōs graphē*," *ZSR* 82 (1965). It has become fashionable to attribute the law of *hybris* to Solon (see N. Fisher, "The Law of *Hubris* in Athens," in *Nomos: Essays in Athenian Law, Politics and Society,* ed. P. Cartledge, P. Millett, and S. Todd [Cambridge: Cambridge University Press, 1990], 123-38, with references in note 2; also O. Murray, "The Solonian Law of *Hubris,*" ibid., 139-45). No Greek text supports this attribution, and the context suggested by Ruschenbusch makes much better sense of the law.

33. Plut. *Sol.* 21.1 = F 32a. Higher payments for insults to the dead and the living are stated in Lex. Cantabr. 671.7 = F 33b; they may reflect later reform of the law.

34. Dem. 21.44; Harpok. s.v. *biaiōn;* Lex. Cantabr. 665.26; cf. Lipsius, *Attisches Recht,* 637-38.

35. Schol. Gen. *Iliad* 21.282 = Solon F 36a; P. Oxy. 221, col. 14.11 = Solon F 36b.

36. [Dem.] 58.19 and 21 (cf. 59.40; Isok. 17.14); cf. above at n. 27.

about the origin of judicial litigation (chap. 4). As will be remembered, the defendant is threatened by the plaintiff's incipient act of self-help and asks a public officer for protection. The officer gives him protection and calls a court into session to judge the issue. If the court finds for the plaintiff, it authorizes him to continue his act of self-help and the officer withdraws protection from the defendant. But a judgment for the plaintiff also implies that the defendant was not entitled to public protection; he exceeded his rights in the request he made of the officer. Therefore the judgment could require him to make amends to the officer.

The *dikē* was the oldest way of proceeding at law in Athens. Only the person whose interests were harmed could initiate a *dikē,* and therefore this suit is sometimes called "the private action." Classical Athens also had other forms of action and in these any citizen not disqualified by *atimia* could initiate proceedings and act as plaintiff. The laws referred to such a person as *ho boulomenos,* "he who wishes (to sue or prosecute)." Among these "public actions" the best attested is the *graphē.* There were also *apagōgē, endeixis,* and *ephēgēsis,* available if the offender was detected committing the offense. The characteristic of *eisangelia* was that *ho boulomenos* made his approach not to an officer but to the council or the assembly. There were other procedures, such as *phasis* and *apographē.* In the second half of the fourth century the Athenians created a new procedure, called *apophasis.* Its characteristic was that the first stage, corresponding to the *anakrisis* of the archon, was a hearing before the Council of the Areopagos. There may have been more varieties of procedure than have been recorded.[37] Each of them had two stages, first a hearing before an officer or body of people to formulate the issue, and then a trial before a *dikastērion* to judge it. For the present purpose of finding whether the Athenians developed a concept of crime it will suffice to consider the *graphē* and *eisangelia.*

Athenian tradition said that Solon had introduced the provision that *ho boulomenos,* the voluntary prosecutor as he is often called, could take action at law for the benefit of persons who had suffered wrongs.[38]

---

37. Several of these procedures are recognized in their distinguishing features by Ruschenbusch, *Untersuchungen,* 64–74. *Apophasis* is known from the scandal concerning Harpalos (Hyper. 5; Dein. 1, 2, 3) and from P. Oxy. 2686.

38. Ar. *AP.* 9.1 = F 40a; cf. G.M. Calhoun, *The Growth of Criminal Law in Ancient Greece* (Berkeley: University of California Press, 1927), 72–87. In a careful study, R. Osborne ("Law in Action in Classical Athens," *JHS* 105 [1985]: 40–58) has noted that an Athenian litigant often had a choice between more than one procedure. He finds that

This provision was the root of the *graphē*. The law offered *graphai*, to be undertaken by a voluntary prosecutor, for many predicaments where the victim himself could not take action. There were *graphai* against harm to an orphan, against harm to an *epiklēros,* and against harm to the estate belonging to an orphan.[39] The orphan, being a minor, and the heiress, being female, could not in person take action at law. The harm might well be inflicted by the guardian who should have protected their interests. Thus nature had not provided a specific person who would take action, and so the law invited the voluntary prosecutor. Again there was a *graphē* against harm to parents.[40] A law of Solon freed a son of the obligation to support his father, if the father had not taught him a craft.[41] If the father taught the son a craft, the father was entitled to support in his old age from the son. If the son did not give him support, the father might be too old and feeble to pursue the case in court, and so the law invited the voluntary prosecutor to take it up. A similar consideration accounts for the *graphai* against the madman and the spendthrift.[42] Those who suffered from the householder's deficiencies were most probably his children; they might well be minors and therefore unable to take action at law.

The action alleging wrongful arrest as an adulterer was noted in chapter 4 (at nn. 31–33). Neither the captor nor the captive could take action, and so the law invited a third party to open proceedings. A *graphē* was provided against anyone who had someone wrongly inscribed as a public debtor,[43] for the victim, being purportedly *atimos,* might be

---

in known cases the plaintiff in a *graphē* often tried to promote his own interests rather than those of the victim of a wrong. He concludes (p. 53): "To bring a *graphē* when one might bring a *dikē* (which might be settled without coming before dikasts) is to bring oneself to public attention." That is true. It does not follow, and Osborne does not say, that the law created *graphai* to enable ambitious men to bring themselves to public attention. To take an extreme and therefore probatory example, it may be that in every occurrence of the *graphē paranomōn,* the plaintiff sought to bring himself to public attention and harm his political rivals. But the *graphē paranomōn* was introduced for the purpose of declaring invalid any decree which conflicted with a law.

39. Ar. *AP.* 56.6.
40. Ar. ibid.
41. Plut. *Sol.* 22.1 = F 56.
42. *Graphē paranoias:* Aischin. 3.251; Ar. *AP.* 56.6. *Graphē argias: kata Nikidou argias* in the index to Lysias; Dem. 57.32; Lex. Cantabr. 665.20; Lex. Seguer. V.310.3; cf. Lipsius, *Attisches Recht,* 353–56.
43. Harpok. s.v. *pseudengraphē;* Suda s.v. *pseudengraphos dikē;* Poll. 8.43; Ar. *AP.* 59.3. The *graphē bouleuseōs* was available if the name was not removed when the debt was paid: *IG* 2². 1631, ll. 385–98; Ar. *AP.* 59.3; cf. Lipsius, *Attisches Recht,* 443–46.

unable to approach a court. A similar consideration accounts for the *graphē pseudoklēteias*. A plaintiff in a *dikē* had to summon the defendant in the presence of witnesses (*klētēres*). If the defendant did not come, the court gave judgment against him in default, provided that witnesses testified to the summons. If a litigant alleged that his adversary had defaulted and produced witnesses who gave false testimony to this effect, the other party might suffer an adverse judgment and might in consequence be unable to seek a remedy at law.[44]

In all these actions, the reason for inviting the voluntary prosecutor to open proceedings was the certain or probable inability of the victim to take action. The reason did not arise from any public interest in the case.[45] The same may be true of the *graphē hybreōs*, the action against injury to the person. The law authorizing this action began with the words:

> If anyone commits outrage against anyone, whether against a child or a woman or a man, from among free persons or slaves, or does anything unlawful to any of these....[46]

The victim might be a child, a woman, or a slave, and would therefore be unable to open proceedings. Admittedly the parent or guardian of a child and the guardian (*kyrios*) of a woman could take action, as could the owner of a slave. But it is easy to imagine circumstances that might impede or delay the guardian, whereas if a man himself were the victim of outrage, he was present and had a direct incentive to act. This consideration accounts for the order in which the law envisages prospective free victims ("a child or a woman or a man").

On the other hand *eisangelia* and some *graphai* were employed against deeds that inflicted harm on the community of Athenian citizens. A law quoted by Hypereides provided for *eisangelia* against offenses of three kinds:

1. subversion of the constitution,
2. betrayal of a city or warships or armed forces,

---

44. Ar. *AP.* 59.3; Poll. 8.44. There was a *graphē pseudomartyriōn* (against false testimony) for a similar reason: Andok. 1.7; cf. Antiph. 5.95 (doubted by Lipsius, *Attisches Recht*, 448, 778 n. 2).
45. Cf. Ruschenbusch, *Untersuchungen*, 53, cf. 48.
46. Dem. 21.47. On the extensive scope of this action see Ruschenbusch, "*Hybreōs graphē*."

3. if an orator in return for bribes did not give the best advice to the assembly.[47]

These activities were penalized because they threatened the community. They did not necessarily or primarily inflict harm on a particular person. So they do not embody the modern concept of crime, which treats harm inflicted on a particular person as if it harmed or threatened the community. Recognition of the offenses for which *eisangelia* was appropriate shows that the citizens of Athens had learned to regard themselves as a community with common interests. To achieve communal self-consciousness was a significant step, and something can be ascertained about the time when the Athenians accomplished it. In the fourth century B.C., subversion was conceived as "overthrow (*katalysis*) of the demos." But an earlier law, quoted by Aristotle, imposed *atimia* on anyone who tried to set up a tyranny.[48] Without giving a precise date, Aristotle cites the law in a sixth-century context and calls it *thesmia*. Whatever its date of origin, it probably figured among the laws of Solon. It may mark the first emergence of communal consciousness.

In the fourth century Athens had many *graphai* against activities that harmed the state.[49] They included the actions against proposing an illegal decree (*graphē paranomōn*) and against proposing an inexpedient law (*graphē nomon mē epitēdeion theinai*).[50] Some were directed against public officers or men performing public tasks. These included the action concerning bribery (*graphē dōrōn*),[51] the action against offenses committed on embassies (*graphē parapresbeias*),[52] the action for embezzling public

---

47. Hyper. 4.7-8. The procedure has had much discussion. One of the questions in dispute is whether *eisangelia* was only available for the stated offenses or also for others; see P.J. Rhodes, "Eisangelia at Athens," *JHS* 99 (1979): 103-14 (arguing for a "non-specific strand" in the law); M.H. Hansen, "Eisangelia in Athens: A reply," *JHS* 100 (1980): 89-95; cf. R. Sealey, "Ephialtes, *Eisangelia* and the Council," in G.S. Shrimpton and D.J. McCargar, eds., *Classical Contributions: Studies in Honour of M.F. McGregor* (Locust Valley, N.Y.: Augustin, 1981), 125-34.

48. Ar. *AP.* 16.10 = Solon F 37a. It is another question, whether the alleged law of Solon about *eisangelia* (*AP.* 8.4 = F 37b) is authentic. Material on Athenian legislation against subversion has been collected by M. Ostwald, "The Athenian Legislation against Tyranny and Subversion," *TAPhA* 86 (1955): 103-28.

49. Many are listed by Lipsius, *Attisches Recht*, 383-420. Little is known about some of them, such as the *graphē prytanikē,* the *graphē proedrikē,* and the *graphē epistatikē.* There may have been more kinds of *graphē* than are attested.

50. Ar. *AP.* 59.2.

51. Ar. *AP.* 54.2; Dem. 21.113; cf. [Dem.] 46.26.

52. Dem. 19.126, 131, 278-80; Aischin. 2.94.

funds (*graphē klopēs dēmosiōn chrēmatōn*),⁵³ and the action for embezzling sacred funds (*graphē klopēs hierōn chrēmatōn*).⁵⁴ The public action against impiety (*graphē asebeias*) protected the community, which might suffer if it tolerated deeds inviting divine punishment.⁵⁵ Again, the action against an alien who passed himself off as a citizen (*graphē xenias*)⁵⁶ protected the community, for encroachment by aliens could diminish the value of citizenship.

In modern societies offenses against the community, such as treason, subversion, and betraying official secrets, are treated as crimes. But some offenses against particular persons, such as theft and bodily injury, are also treated as crimes, although it is not obvious that they harm the community. They are treated as crimes on the basis of a legal fiction, which says that the community is harmed by deeds that disturb its peace. Criminal proceedings have to extend the notion of public peace, sometimes to a large degree. It is relatively easy to classify bodily injury to a particular person as a threat to the public peace. It is more difficult to bring theft under the same classification. The Athenians did not adopt the legal fiction underlying strictly criminal proceedings. They recognized communal interests and protected them with actions that the voluntary prosecutor could open. But deeds harming the interests of particular persons were treated as delicts, not crimes, and the voluntary prosecutor was only invited to act if the victim could not do so.

To say this is not to pass any judgment of value on Athenian procedure. Moreover, it would not be legitimate to regard the modern law of crime as a goal toward which ancient societies were developing. Historical study does not provide grounds for a teleological view of human development.⁵⁷ Instead it should be recognized that different societies

---

53. Dem. 24.112, cf. 127; Ar. *AP.* 54.2.
54. Dem. 19.293. The relation of this to embezzlement of public funds and to sacrilege (*hierosylia*) is not wholly clear; for discussion see D. Cohen, *Theft in Athenian Law* (Munich: Beck, 1983), 49–51, 93–115.
55. Ar. *AP.* 57.2; cf. Lipsius, *Attisches Recht,* 358–68.
56. Lys. 13.60; Isai. 3.37; Dem. 24.131; 39.18; *Ep.* 3.29; [Dem.] 40.41; 49.66; Ar. *AP.* 59.3 (noting also the *graphē dōroxenias*).
57. Such a view vitiates the valuable work of Calhoun, *The Growth of Criminal Law.* Thus he wrote: "The notion of a wrong to the community must be extended to include many acts at first regarded solely as offenses against the individual, and the processes by which the community punishes must be developed and adapted to the adequate protection of all rights, private as well as public, which enter into this enlarged conception of public peace and good order" (pp. 4–5; cf. his use of the expressions "primitive," pp. 2 and 5, and "true criminal law," p. 3).

adopt different ways of dealing with activities that they recognize as wrongs. Each way of proceeding has its own merits and defects. Criminal proceedings, for example, do not necessarily protect the interests of the victim; they preserve the peace by preventing him from retaliating, and they are more efficient in pursuing this aim than in deterring criminals. Possibly it could be maintained that a law of crime suits a large industrial society and a law of delict befits a smaller community with a simpler economy. But perhaps that judgment would be premature.

CHAPTER 6

To Each His Due

Athenian Procedure Refined

This essay began by recognizing a semantic field, represented in English by the words *law, justice,* and *right.* In other modern languages the same field can readily be recognized, although no single word may be coextensive, and no more than coextensive, in meaning with any of the English words: *Recht* may sometimes need to be rendered by *law* and sometimes by *right.* National differences in the components that constitute the common semantic field are doubtless due to differences of intellectual history. The essay set out to discover the historical contribution of Greek thought to the field of law, justice, and right. It hoped to discover principles, concepts, and aims that underlay the development of law in Greek cities.

Attention was directed in chapter 2 to compilations of laws. It was maintained that codes of prescriptive law were a Greek invention, although the Hittite laws came close to fulfilling the same role. It was also maintained that the adoption of written compilations of laws was an experience common to many Greek cities and shaped the Greek concept of law; Greeks believed that the acknowledged laws had provided in advance for some occurrences, but other occurrences fell into gaps between the laws and were to be decided by the judge or judges at discretion, if dispute should arise.

Pursuing the theme of unity of concepts, aims, and principles, chapter 3 considered substantive law in different Greek cities. It concluded by recognizing the underlying concept of the fully privileged member of the community. Apart from adult male citizens, a Greek community could have other people—women, children, aliens, and slaves—who might be numerous, and at least some of them were necessary to communal survival. But only adult male citizens could exercise the privileges of membership in the community to their fullest extent. In Greek thought citizenship was a privileged status, whereas in Roman thought it was relatively egalitarian, for it was possessed in full extent by women, conceded to slaves on manumission, and granted by the assembled Romans and even by military commanders to whole communities. The question has still to be answered, how the concept of a fully privileged member of the community arose, and answering it will be one of the tasks of the present chapter.

This chapter looks for the original impulse that prompted Greeks to develop legal institutions. In preparation chapters 4 and 5 considered matters of procedural law. It has become apparent that Greeks in general, and Athenians in particular, gave a good deal of thought to developing the field of law, justice, and right. They were assiduous in elaborating procedures to protect the substantive rights belonging within that field. This conclusion can be strengthened by noting two innovations of the fourth century B.C. in Athenian procedure. These were *paragraphē* and institutionalized arbitration.

The treaty which ended the civil war of 403 B.C. included a provision of amnesty, "that no one should be permitted to enter a plea against anyone on account of past events, except against the Thirty and the Ten and the Eleven and those who had governed the Peiraieus, and not even against these once they rendered accounts."[1] But a prohibition may be ineffectual unless a procedure is added to uphold it. A law was passed, probably in 401/0 B.C., creating the procedure of *paragraphē* to uphold the prohibition against actions arising from occurrences of the time of revolution and civil war. If a plaintiff opened an action, the defendant could reply at the preliminary hearing (*anakrisis*) before the public officer by asserting that the matter alleged by the plaintiff was covered by the amnesty and therefore not admissible to judgment. This plea by the defendant was called a *paragraphē*. There were now two sets of putative facts confronting the public officer, namely the original complaint of the plaintiff and the defendant's reply to the effect that the matter in dispute arose from the conditions of revolution and civil war. Either set of alleged

---

1. Ar. *AP.* 39.6. Isok. 18.20 makes the implied reference to forensic procedures explicit; cf. Andok. 1.90–91; P.J. Rhodes, *A Commentary on the Aristotelian "Athenaion Politeia"* (Oxford: Oxford University Press, 1981), 468–69; M. Chambers, *Aristoteles: Staat der Athener* (Berlin: Akademie Verlag, 1990), 318–19.

facts might be true or false. The effect of the *paragraphē* was that the officer called a *dikastērion* into session to judge first the truth of the defendant's allegation. At this hearing the original defendant spoke first; the original plaintiff had an opportunity to reply and to try to show that the matter was not covered by the amnesty. If the court at this hearing found that the matter was indeed covered by the amnesty and therefore not admissible, the lawsuit was at an end. But if the court found that the original complaint was admissible, it met in a second session to determine the truth or falsehood of that complaint.[2]

Later, at times and in circumstances that are not recorded, laws were passed recognizing other reasons why a plaintiff's plea should not be admitted to judgment. The defendant might respond to a plaintiff's plea by saying that the question had already been determined in an earlier trial or in an act of arbitration that both parties had accepted. As no official records of trials or of arbitration were kept, the truth or falsehood of such a response could only be ascertained from testimony of witnesses. Again, the defendant might respond to the plaintiff's plea by saying that a period of limitation had expired. The period attested for Athens is five years. In short, for any of several reasons recognized by the laws, a defendant might deny the admissibility of the plaintiff's plea. Consequently the *dikastērion* heard first the *paragraphē,* the allegation denying admissibility. If it found that this allegation was not factually grounded, it proceeded in a second session to hear the plaintiff's original complaint.[3]

Paragraphē came to be widely used in the fourth century B.C. No fewer than nine extant speeches were composed for cases of this kind.[4] To appreciate its distinctively Athenian character one must recognize the general problem that it served to solve. When a dispute begins, the parties often argue at cross-purposes. The plaintiff says that the defendant has infringed the plaintiff's right, and the defendant does not admit or deny

---

2. Isok. 18.2–3; H.J. Wolff: *Die attische Paragraphe. Ein Beitrag zum Problem der Auflockerung archaischer Prozessformen* (Weimar: Böhlau, 1966), 87–89. On the date see D.M. MacDowell, "The Chronology of Athenian Speeches and Legal Innovations in 401–398 B.C.," *RIDA,* 3d ser., 18 (1971): 267–73.

3. Wolff (n. 2 above) 89–105. For the allegation that the dispute had already been judged or determined by arbitration see Dem. 36.25; 37.19–20; [Dem.] 38.5; cf. Dem. 24.54; Poll. 8.57. For the general limitation of five years, see Dem. 36.26; it is attested specifically for claims of orphans against guardians: [Dem.] 38.17. A limitation of unspecified length is mentioned by [Dem.] 43.16 and Poll. 8.57.

4. Isok. 18; Lys. 23; Dem. 32–38.

the plaintiff's allegation but raises some further issue. Before the dispute can be submitted to a body of judges, who will decide which party is right, the two litigants must be induced to argue about the same thing. That is, the issue between them must be joined; it must be formulated in a single, sometimes complex, proposition for the one to assert and the other to deny. At Athens before the fourth century, joinder of the issue was brought about in the preliminary hearing (*anakrisis*) before the public officer. This hearing concluded with the *antōmosia;* that is, the plaintiff asserted his plea on oath and the defendant denied it on oath.[5] *Paragraphē,* when employed, took the burden of joining the issue from the officer and entrusted it to the *dikastērion* at its first session. Thus the role of the officer was diminished, or in Athenian terms, the preliminary hearing before him changed from *anakrisis* to *proanakrisis*.[6]

Comparison and contrast with Roman procedure are instructive. In the formulary procedure a case went through two stages, proceedings *in iure* and proceedings *apud iudicem*. At the first stage the parties appeared before the praetor. The latter listened to the quarrel and stated the issue in dispute by drawing up a formula. This was an instruction to the judge, whom the praetor also appointed. The formula told the judge to find for the plaintiff, if on inquiry he discovered that the plaintiff's allegation appeared to be true; otherwise he was to absolve the defendant. The formula could be complex; it could, for example, comprise an *exceptio,* such as a plea of the defendant in bar of action, and a *replicatio* or answer of the plaintiff.[7] Thus joinder of the issue was achieved by the praetor, and it remained for the *iudex* to inquire into the facts at the second stage of the trial.

The praetor had considerable power of discretion in drawing up formulas. The edict that he issued when he entered office included clauses stating circumstances in which he would "grant an action" (*iudicium dare*), and the *lex Cornelia* of 67 required praetors to observe their edicts.[8] If a dispute not foreseen in the edict was brought to the praetor, he could accept it, devising a new formula, or reject it, as he thought fit;

---

5. Plat. *Apol.* 19b, 24b; Isai. 3.6; 5.2 and 4; 9.1; cf. J.H. Lipsius, *Das attische Recht und Rechtsverfahren,* 3 vols. (Leipzig, Reisland, 1905-15), 830 with further references.

6. Ar. *AP.* 3.5; cf. R. Sealey, *The Athenian Republic: Democracy or the Rule of Law?* (University Park: Pennsylvania State University Press, 1987), 68-69.

7. B. Nicholas, *An Introduction to Roman Law* (Oxford: Oxford University Press, 1962), 24-25. The formula could be still more elaborate with *duplicatio* and *triplicatio:* Gaius 4.126-129.

8. Asconius 59C; Dio. 36.40.1-2.

he could seek advice from jurisconsults. The praetor was a more authoritarian figure than an Athenian officer. The procedure of *paragraphē* allowed for pleas in bar of action but was relatively rigid; an action could only be barred for a reason recognized in the laws. Because the praetor had greater authority, he could develop the law with more flexibility.

The other innovation calling for note created means to encourage settlement of disputes out of court by arbitration. Doubtless disputants of mild disposition had submitted their differences to third persons by agreement in hope of help toward settlement from time immemorial. Indeed procedure within a *dikastērion* offered little scope for negotiation. The *dikastai* listened to the uninterrupted speeches of the two parties and then cast their votes on the basis of the impression made on them by the presentations as a whole; within the courtroom there was no stage at which particular issues could be argued back and forth. Before a private suit came into court there could be numerous meetings of the parties, usually with companions, and at these meetings particular points within each side's case could be challenged or defended and negotiations could take place.[9] The need for informal hearing of private cases was met by a law, passed probably in 400/399 B.C., to institute public arbitrators.[10]

In consequence of the new law, the parties to many private suits went first to a member of the board called the Forty or the Forty Judges, four members being chosen from each of the *phylai*. These officers had authority to determine suits where the value at stake was not more than ten drachmas, but they forwarded other cases to arbitrators. Male citizens were required to serve as arbitrators when they were in their sixtieth year. On receiving a case the arbitrator tried to bring the parties to a settlement. The proceedings were informal, and it was in the interests of each party to bring his witnesses and any documents on which he could draw to support his case. If both parties agreed to the recommendation of the arbitrator, the suit was at an end. But if either of them rejected the recommendation and decided to take the dispute to court, the documents

---

9. G. Thür, "Komplexe Prozessführung dargestellt am Beispiel des Trapezitikos (Isokr. 17)," *Symposion 1971* (Cologne: Böhlau, 1975), 157–88.

10. Information on the arbitrators is provided by Ar. *AP.* 53; cf. Rhodes, *Commentary,* 587–96; Chambers, *Staat,* 378–80. The date of their introduction is discussed by MacDowell (n. 2 above); he suggests that the law was passed in 400/399 B.C. and the first body of arbitrators served in 399/8 B.C.

of the two parties, including the statements of their witnesses, were put into two vessels. These were sealed and the arbitrator attached his recommendation. He sent the parties to the four members of the Forty who were drawn from the phyle of the defendant. These four then brought the case before a *dikastērion,* which had 201 *dikastai* if the value in dispute did not exceed 1,000 drachmas but otherwise 401 *dikastai.* In the ensuing trial the parties were not allowed to draw on testimony or documents other than those contained in the sealed vessels. The institutionalization of arbitration had the incidental consequence that henceforth testimony was presented in court in writing; previously it had been given orally. That change came about by 389 B.C.[11]

Enough has been said to show that the Athenians gave a great deal of thought to developing substantive and procedural law. But the Greeks, unlike the Romans, did not compose a body of juristic literature. So the type of thought embodied in Greek law is relatively inarticulate. It is to be ascertained, not from the writings of philosophers or jurists, but from the language employed in transactions and litigation. To discover the starting point for the growth of Greek law one must go back to key words of normative force as employed in the *Iliad* and the *Odyssey.*

Homeric *Dikē* Again

An earlier chapter (4) recognized *dikē* in a procedural sense. It was a mode of proof. Law in its most comprehensive scope can be regarded in each of two ways. On the one hand it is a system of rights, and actions are the means devised to uphold them. On the other, it is a system of actions, and when an action is made available it generates a right. On the whole the former view is modern and the other is Roman. Yet the difference is only one of emphasis.[12] The question of the relative priority of procedural and substantive law is ultimately a chicken-and-

---

11. On the date see E. Ruschenbusch, "Drei Beiträge zur öffentlichen Diaita in Athen," *Symposion 1982* (Cologne: Böhlau, 1985), 31–40, at 34–35, with references to previous discussions. Ruschenbusch derives a *terminus ante quem* for the change to written testimony from Isai. 5.2. He tries also to derive a *terminus post quem* from Lys. 16.3, a speech belonging within the years 392–387 B.C. But the latter speech was delivered at a *dokimasia* before the council; possibly the older custom of oral testimony continued in hearings before the council after it had been abandoned in the courts in consequence of arbitration.

12. Nicholas, *Introduction to Roman Law,* 20. Likewise in the early stages of the Common Law writs generated rights; cf. D. Henrich, *Einführung in das englische Privatrecht,* 2d ed. (Darmstadt: Wissenschaftliche Buchgesellschaft, 1993), 3.

egg question; when a Roman praetor created a new formula, he did so because he wished to uphold a right that he thereby recognized. Even so, the Roman view offers help toward understanding the Homeric poems. For as has been seen, the *Iliad* portrays procedures for the peaceful settlement of disputes, but the poems have no knowledge of written laws. Without the fixity of writing substantive rights are likely to be fluid.

Yet *dikē* in the Homeric poems can have a substantive sense. At many points in the *Odyssey* someone's behavior is reported and an explanation is added by saying that such is the *dikē* of people of a specified kind. Expressions employing the word *dikē* in this manner may be distinguished into three types.

1. The *dikē* may be a right.
When Odysseus finds his elderly father laboring in the orchard, he expresses surprise. As he says, Laertes looks like a man who could well sleep on a soft bed after washing and eating; "for that is the *dikē* of old men" (24.254-55). Again, earlier in the poem, Penelope says that Odysseus never did or uttered anything arbitrary in Ithaka, even though it is the *dikē* of *basilēes* to hate or love people according to their whim (4.690-92). Likewise, when Odysseus and Telemachos have removed the weapons from the halls of the palace, the younger man notices that the walls and pillars are shining as with fire; he suspects that there must be a god within. His father bids him be silent, for such is the *dikē* of gods (19.42-43). That is, gods are entitled to behave in astonishing ways and men should not presume to ask questions.

2. The *dikē* may be a duty.
Only one passage suggests this sense. When Penelope shows herself in splendor to the suitors and solicits gifts from them, she upbraids them, saying:

> This has not been the *dikē* of suitors in the past, when they wish to woo a woman of merit, the daughter of a rich man, and they compete with one another. They themselves bring cattle and fat sheep as a feast for the bride's people and they give splendid gifts, but they do not consume another man's livelihood with impunity. (18.275-80)

Possibly it is excessive to discover a sense of duty in the word *dikē* here.

Perhaps Penelope's meaning is not that suitors in general have a duty to bring cattle and gifts but that her actual suitors have no right to consume another man's livelihood. Even so, her words show how a negated statement of a right could approach to a positive statement of a duty.

3. The *dikē* may be an actual condition.

Eumaios, offering hospitality to the disguised Odysseus, apologizes because what he can offer amounts to little. "For this is the *dikē* of serfs, who live in constant fear when young masters are in control" (14.59-61). Again, Odysseus in disguise yields to Penelope's demand that he tell her his origin, and he says that the telling will add to his sorrows. For the *dikē* is that a man should suffer sorrows when he is away from his native land for a long time (19.168-70). Likewise, when Odysseus has called up the ghost of his mother from the underworld, he tries to embrace her but he cannot. He wonders whether Persephone has sent a mere image to increase his grief. But his mother corrects him:

> Alas, my child, wretched above all men, Persephone, the daughter of Zeus, does not trick thee. But this is the *dikē* of mortals, when one has died. The sinews no longer have flesh or bones, but those parts are subdued by the mighty power of burning fire, once the breath has left the white bones and the ghost has taken wing and flown away like a dream. (11.216-22)

In occurrences of all three types *dikē* can be rendered by *portion*. That is, some of the ramified usages of the Greek word coincide with some of the ramified usages of the English word. In all three types *dikē* is the behavior or condition of people of a specified kind, whether they be old men, serfs, suitors, or the dead. People of every kind have a proper place in the order of the universe, that is, in the society of men and gods. So even when *dikē* is an actual condition, it is implied to be legitimate, since it is part of an order that is above challenge. The condition of serfs or of the dead may be sad, but it is justified by the cosmic order in which it belongs. *Dikē* in the substantive usage under consideration is never merely descriptive but always normative.

In an inquiry into Greek justice, L.R. Palmer recognized a "semantic field" and the place of *dikē* within it.¹³ The field included words meaning boundaries, limits of time and place, marks as characteristics, and marks as aims. It embraced words for throwing, for pointing out, for measuring, judging, and saying. It comprised ideas of the opportune moment, of the season, of the year, moreover of distribution, apportionment, wealth, fortune, and fate. Many words from many roots functioned within the field. *Dikē* as a boundary-mark had its place together with *deiknymi*, "to point out." The Greek vocabulary belonging to this field proved to be rich and informative. Palmer was also able to trace words belonging to the same field in many other Indo-European languages or groups of languages (Germanic, Celtic, Latin, Slavic, Baltic, Albanian, Indo-Iranian). The words within the field have a normative aspect.

Within Indo-Iranian thought Palmer noted the belief in a primordial act of distribution that produced the universe and society. From the *Iliad*, one may call to mind a remark of Poseidon, made when Iris has brought him an order from Zeus:

> For shame! In spite of his worth he has spoken an insolent utterance, if he will restrict me by force against my will, although I am his equal in prestige. For being begotten by Kronos, we are three brothers, whom Rhea bore, Zeus and I and as the third Hades, who rules those dwelling below. Everything has been distributed into three parts, and each of us has received his share of honor. When lots were cast, it fell to me to dwell forever in the grey sea; Hades received the misty darkness, and Zeus received the broad heaven in the sky and the clouds. The earth and wide Olympos are common to us all. (15.185-93)

This tale of a primordial division of the universe between three divine brothers presupposes the preoccupation of Homeric thought with just distribution. Doubtless it mirrors occurrences among men, when booty or land was to be distributed after warfare. The question of apportionment arose regularly at communal meals; indeed the Germanic word *meal* has a secure place within Palmer's semantic field.

A further word needs to be brought into relation to that field. Poseidon said that he was "equal in prestige" to Zeus (*homotimos*) and that each

---

13. L.R. Palmer, "The Indo-European Origins of Greek Justice," *Transactions of the Philological Society* (1950): 149-68.

of the brothers had received his share of "honor" (*timē*). In Greek thought *timē* carries as heavy a burden of meaning as *love* for the Christian.

Homeric *Timē*

The noun *timē*, with the related verbs (*tinein, timān, atimān*), occurs frequently in the epics. It means the esteem in which someone is held,[14] and the verbs mean to pay honor to someone.[15] Often the honor is expressed by material gifts or payments. The kings in Lykia are honored with thrones and superior shares of meat and wine, Achilles honors Nestor with a prize at the competitive games in which he has not competed, and hosts honor their guests with hospitality and with gifts.[16] Material treatment is indicated when parents are said to honor illegitimate children equally or almost equally with the legitimate.[17] The verb can mean to cause people to honor someone. Patroklos exhorts the Myrmidones to fight well in order to bring honor to Achilles.[18] After Agamemnon has dishonored Achilles by taking Briseis from him, much is said about the prospect that Zeus will cause the Achaians or Agamemnon in particular to honor Achilles.[19]

Timē comes from Zeus.[20] A greater degree of *timē* belongs to gods[21] and to kings[22] than to others. But others, bards for example,[23] have their proper share of *timē*. When a stranger visits the island of the Phaiakians, each of the leaders of the community has his share in the honor (*timē*) of entertaining him.[24] In an important sense the epic order of gods and men is a classless society. Each member of the community has his stand-

---

14. *Il.* 4.410; 9.319; 9.514.
15. *Il.* 1.174-75; 9.38; 16.460; 23.788; *Od.* 3.379; 5.36; 7.67-72. Even in the middle form, the verb can have active force: *Il.* 22.233-37; *Od.* 19.280=23.339; 20.129.
16. *Il.* 12.310-11; 23.649; *Od.* 19.280-82; 20.129-33; 23.339-41.
17. *Od.* 14.203; 15.365.
18. *Il.* 16.271; cf. 16.84.
19. *Il.* 1.505-10; 1.558-59; 2.3-4; 8.372; 15.77. Gods cause people to honor other mortals at *Il.* 15.610-12; 17.99.
20. *Il.* 2.197; cf. 1.352-56; 9.608.
21. *Il.* 9.498.
22. *Il.* 1.278-79; 17.248-51. Often the *timē* of a king is his kingdom or royal office: *Il.* 20.179-81; *Od.* 1.115-17; 11.494-97, cf. 503; 24.30-31. The king of Lykia gave Bellerophon "half of all the royal *timē*," *Il.* 6.193; cf. 9.616.
23. *Od.* 8.479-81.
24. *Od.* 11.338.

ing (*timē*) in it, not because he belongs to a recognized class, but because of his individual quality. Leukothea used to be a mortal but now in the sea she has received her share of *timē* from the gods.[25] The poet recognizes her, not as a member of any class of marine goddesses, but as a unique being having her own *timē,* her distinctive place in the order of the universe. Kastor and Polydeukes beneath the earth have *timē* from Zeus, alternating between life and death; their *timē* is equal to that of gods.[26] Like Leukothea, they have a unique condition.

Descent can be decisive in determining the *timē* due to a mortal. When the king of Lykia recognized that Bellerophon was "the offspring of a god," he gave him his daughter and half of his kingdom.[27] Early in the twenty-fourth book of the *Iliad* Apollo reproaches the gods because they have not saved the corpse of Hektor from Achilles. Hera retorts with indignation:

Such would be thy word, god of the silver bow, if thou shouldst assign like *timē* to Achilles and Hektor! Hektor is mortal and he sucked the breast of a woman, but Achilles is the child of a goddess and I myself nursed her and reared her and gave her as wife to a man, Peleus, who was loved dearly by the immortals. All you gods came to attend the wedding. Thou too, though a companion of evil ones and ever faithless, wert among them at the feast with thy lyre.[28]

Each man's *timē* is his inherent quality. It reflects his descent and it is reflected in his deeds and in the esteem that people accord him.

If one man takes what belongs to another, he disregards the latter's *timē*. Retaliation is an attempt to recover *timē*. After Paris had taken Helen to Troy, the Achaians went on an expedition "to win *timē* for Menelaos."[29] The payment to be made by the aggressor is far more than a mere refund of the value of the thing taken. At Ithaka, when the fight

---

25. *Od.* 5.334–35.
26. *Od.* 11.302–4.
27. *Il.* 6.191–93.
28. *Il.* 24.56–63. The response of Zeus is memorable (ll. 66–70): the *timē* to be accorded to the two men will not be the same, but Hektor too was most dear to the gods, for he offered large sacrifices. Likewise, at 1.352–54, Achilles says that Zeus ought to have assured him *timē* because of the identity of his mother.
29. *Il.* 1.159. Variations on the same theme of recovering *timē* for Menelaos occur at *Il.* 3.284–91; 3.458–59; 5.552–53; 17.92; *Od.* 14.70.

in the hall of the palace has begun and Odysseus has shot down Antinoos, Eurymachos proposes a settlement. In the course of his speech he says:

> Spare thy people. But afterwards we will levy a contribution in the land in atonement for what has been eaten and drunk in thy palace, we will each of us bring together a *timē* in a value of twenty oxen, and thus we will repay thee bronze and gold until thy heart is appeased. (*Od.* 22.54–59)

Here Eurymachos suggests that each suitor should provide a *timē* in a large value in addition to making good the losses inflicted on the property of Odysseus. An offender does not merely inflict loss. By inflicting material loss he challenges the standing (*timē*) of his victim in the community, and to restore the *status quo ante facinus* he must both repay the loss and hand over plentiful valuables (*timē*).

In Homeric thought the order of the universe embraces gods and men. Within that order each has his own place because of his inherent quality. But that is not the whole truth about the world of Homeric fantasy. The poets constructed that world as an extension of the society they knew. What they knew was a multitude of Greek communities, varying in size and stability and bounded by an expanse of hazards and monsters, such as Odysseus encountered in his wanderings. Within each small community, within each embryonic *polis,* a man's *timē* had to be recognized; at least, if it were flouted, trouble was likely to ensue. Communal ties could be extended beyond the single *polis*. A traveler equipped with gifts for exchange might visit a land where he or his father was known to men of power, and he would be welcomed. But the unknown wanderer who came to the community from outside had no *timē*. He was at the mercy of anyone who met him. Nausikaa and Eumaios, being persons of high principles, said that all strangers and beggars are from Zeus.[30] They had no human protector. Therefore, when Agamemnon took away the prize awarded to Achilles, the latter expressed his pain by saying that Agamemnon had treated him "like a wanderer who has no *timē*."[31] The Greeks for whom the Homeric poets sang valued *timē* because some men had none; they were outsiders.

---

30. *Od.* 6.207–8; 14.57–58.
31. *Il.* 9.648; 16.59.

Mesopotamian Justice

Homeric *timē* is the sum of a man's rights. Moreover each man's *timē* is distinctive. It inheres in him in consequence of his own quality, in which descent is one among several factors. Society as imagined in the Homeric poems consists not of classes but of single persons, each one differing from the next. *Timē* evidently plays a part in the semantic field recognized by Palmer; its meaning is not unlike that of *dikē* in the substantive sense. The same semantic field, in which a concept of apportionment is central, can be discerned in many Indo-European languages. The ideas constituting the field are richly attested in extant Greek literature. They may have developed to moderately different results in different societies, but they must have been present in some form in the parent of the different languages. So the question should be asked, whether ideas belonging to this semantic field, ideas such as *dikē* and *timē,* are strictly an Indo-European heritage or have their counterparts in the early societies of the Near East.

Knowledge of law and legal procedure in Mesopotamia of the Bronze Age is derived from documents of various kinds, including contracts, royal letters, and above all records of trials. As remarked in chapter 2, records of lawsuits have been studied intensively for two periods, namely the Neo-Sumerian, marked by the Third Dynasty of Ur, and the Old Babylonian, marked by the First Dynasty of Babylon.[32] In each of these periods a single city (Ur, Babylon) tried to bring all the cities of Lower Mesopotamia under its rule and was successful for a considerable time. The documents studied are limited in date and place; for example, the Neo-Sumerian material comes from a period of forty-nine years and belongs to an archive in which records of lawsuits from different cities, all within the province of Lagash, were stored.[33] Unlike the so-called codes of law, which were considered previously, the records of lawsuits reflect the actual administration of justice. Judges decided cases, not on the basis of the codes, but in conformity with what they considered equitable.[34]

---

32. A. Walther, *Das altbabylonische Gerichtswesen* (Leipzig: Hinrichs, 1917); J.G. Lautner, *Die richterliche Entscheidung und die Streitbeendigung im altbabylonischen Prozessrechte* (Leipzig: Weicher, 1922); A. Falkenstein, *Die neusumerischen Gerichtsurkunden 1: Einleitung und systematische Darstellung* (Munich: Bayerische Akademie der Wissenschaften, 1956).

33. Falkenstein, *Neusumerische Gerichtsurkunden 1:* 1-18.

34. Walther, *Altbabylonisches Gerichtswesen*, 227.

The archive containing the Neo-Sumerian records of lawsuits was probably kept by the *ensi* (prince of the city), who governed Lagash and its neighborhood.[35] It is presumed that the purpose in collecting the records into an archive was to put the administration of justice on a firmer basis. Often the record of a lawsuit has the heading *di-til-la,* "final judgment." The word is first attested on an Old Akkadian document, but it is Sumerian and so it must have been transmitted from the early Dynastic period (ca. 3000–ca. 2370 B.C.).

The picture of judicial administration reconstructed from these documents is highly monarchical. The king administered justice. Urnammu, the founder of the Third Dynasty, said in a hymn: "My judicial utterance brought Sumer and Akkad on to a single track." The king often deputed judicial authority to his officers and especially to the prince of the city. There is little or no trace of any exercise of judicial competence by temples or local communities. The prince of the city might in turn depute jurisdiction to other officers. Judgment in particular cases could be given by a single judge or by groups numbering up to seven. Judges were chosen from people of high rank in society and administration. Records of many lawsuits name at the end another officer significant in the procedure; that is the *mashkim* or commissary. When a plaintiff addressed himself to the prince of the city, the latter could appoint a commissary to conduct a preliminary inquiry into the case. The commissary, like the judge, was chosen from people of high rank.

When a case came into court, various methods of proof were employed. They included interrogation of experts or of persons called "old people," testimony of witnesses without oath, testimony of witnesses on oath, the oath of a party, and proof by documents. Oaths were of two kinds, promissory and assertory (sometimes purgatorial, cf. chap. 4). In a promissory oath the person swearing undertook to do something. He swore by the name of the king or by the life of the king. Such an oath could be sworn anywhere. In an assertory oath the person swearing said that something was true and asked a god to inflict harm on him if he uttered a falsehood. An assertory oath could only be sworn in a temple.[36]

---

35. This and the ensuing paragraphs on the Neo-Sumerian material are based on Falkenstein, *Neusumerische Gerichtsurkunden 1:* 7–80.

36. The student of Greek procedure will recall that Plangon identified the father of her two sons by an assertory oath sworn in the Delphinion: [Dem.] 40.11. The requirement of assertory oaths (*antōmosia*) from the parties may explain why trials before the ephetai

The judgments that concluded proceedings in court were of two kinds, conditional and definitive. A conditional judgment required one or more persons to swear an assertory oath. Then the participants left the court and went to a temple. If a party refused to swear the assertory oath required of him, he lost his case. The reader of the *Iliad* will remember the oath tendered to Antilochos by Menelaos. But sometimes the court issued a definitive judgment. This was often a brief statement in the passive voice with the form: "The thing was adjudicated to A." Occasionally the record says that the judgment was an act of the king or of the prince of the city. Sometimes the reason for the judgment is given in the record, and the character of the stated reasons is worth attention. Examples are: "because A had sworn an oath by the king to B," "because A had robbed him," "because A was killed," "because A had stolen B's bed," "because A had inflicted damage on the field," "because they had taken this barley for themselves," "because he did not deliver these fish to the palace." The explicit reasons are not general rules but the circumstances of the particular case. The Sumerian judge did not ground his judgment in any acknowledged laws, as a modern judge does. Admittedly any act of adjudication may presuppose some concept, however vague and variable, of a norm, but that is not the same as the conscious application of a recognized law to a case.

Finally the record of a lawsuit sometimes included a declaration of renunciation. That is, the unsuccessful litigant gave up his claim. He swore a promissory oath by the king "not to come back to" the thing in dispute. Probably this practice was devised to facilitate execution of the judgment. It will call for remark in relation to the Old Babylonian material.

In the documents from the First Dynasty of Babylon, as in those of the Neo-Sumerian period, the king is presented as the ultimate source of jurisdiction. He often deputed judicial authority to the *ensi* or other officers as judges. Each case was heard by a small number of judges. Even when only one judge is mentioned, he may have sat as a chairman with colleagues. The king had power to pardon and could depute it to judges. But sometimes justice was administered by a local community or by personnel of temples. The community is probably to be identified

---

were held in temples (Ar. *AP*. 57.3). Likewise the law-code of Gortyn provides for an assertory oath to be sworn in a temple (*IC* 4.72: III, ll. 5–9).

with a judicial body called "the eldest of the city." Sometimes the task of judging a case was assigned to the community by the king. Probably the community was held to derive its judicial authority from the king.[37]

In the temples tasks had become differentiated. At a much earlier period the priest had served in many capacities, as physician, for example, and as judge, and as scribe. By the Old Babylonian period these professions had become specialized within the body of the personnel of the temples. Thus there were temple-judges. Information on court procedure in Old Babylonia extends over some three centuries. Some historians have supposed that as time passed the jurisdiction of the state grew in compass and caused that of the temples to diminish. But there is no suggestion of any conflict or rivalry between different sources of judicial authority. A better view recognizes that the temple-judges did not disappear but came to be integrated into the state system of courts. Possibly they had been so integrated from the start and any changes were merely administrative.[38]

When a case came into court, methods of proof included documents, witnesses, and oaths. As in Neo-Sumerian society, oaths were of two kinds. An assertory oath could only be sworn in a temple, but a promissory oath could be sworn elsewhere. Likewise judgments were of two kinds. The court could find for the plaintiff or for the defendant, or it could formulate an oath and invite a party to swear it.[39]

Often the record of an Old Babylonian lawsuit includes a declaration of renunciation (*tuppu lâ ragāmim*). That is, after a final decision had been reached, the unsuccessful litigant swore, at the invitation of the judges, a promissory oath that he abandoned his claim and would not try to assert it again in future. The regularity with which this renunciation appears in recorded suits has prompted the theory that Old Babylonian procedure was originally voluntary recourse to arbitration. The judgment, it is suggested, did not itself bind the parties but was merely a proposal; this proposal acquired authority only when the parties accepted it and in particular when the losing party agreed to abide by it. This

---

37. For the material of this paragraph see Walther, *Altbabylonisches Gerichtswesen*, 5–105. Lautner, *Richterliche Entscheidung*, 6–35 notes differences of procedure between the royal court and the popular court; officers of the royal court have a larger role in compelling the defendant and witnesses to attend. But these differences need not impair the conclusion reached in this paragraph.

38. Walther, *Altbabylonisches Gerichtswesen*, 180–91.

39. Ibid., 191–95; 212–28; Lautner, *Richterliche Entscheidung*, 25–48.

condition continued supposedly until the growth of royal power brought binding authority to the king's courts.[40]

Against this theory it can be urged that definitive judgments are given in the records of suits in categorical language. The same is true of the Neo-Sumerian material, where declarations of renunciation are less prominent and each record bears the heading *di-til-la,* "final judgment." One would not expect Old Babylonian courts to be less authoritative than those of an earlier period. Besides, as noted in chapter 4, there are serious objections to any theory that tries to derive authoritative jurisdiction from voluntary arbitration. An easier explanation can be offered for the frequency of the declarations of renunciation in Old Babylonian texts. It is one thing to win a lawsuit and another to get the judgment executed. In antiquity the burden of execution usually rested on the shoulders of the winning litigant. The Babylonian declaration of renunciation may have been intended to help the successful litigant toward executing the judgment, even if the defeated adversary should be recalcitrant. Many of the extant records are documents issued to the successful party. The document was his title to the thing in dispute. The reason why the declaration of renunciation is less prominent in the Neo-Sumerian material is that that material comes from the archive of the prince of the city.

The Neo-Sumerian and Old Babylonian material provides many points of suggestive comparison with Greek practice, for example in methods of proof. Note should also be taken of judges who decide without reference to explicit laws; Greeks had judicial procedures for settling disputes before they had any written laws. Judges who have to decide a case without the help of laws reduced to the rigidity of writing are often said to uphold custom or customary law, and although that is true, it can mean that the judges have untrammeled discretion. They decide each case in the light of what seems equitable.

The salient fact about Mesopotamian justice in contrast to Greek practice is its centralized character. The king is the sole source of justice. Other judges exercise authority deputed to them by the king. This condition is fully apparent in the Neo-Sumerian material and it is highly probable for the Old Babylonian records, where jurisdiction by the community or by temple-judges does not necessarily amount to an exception. The despotic character of Mesopotamian society contrasts with Greece.

---

40. This was Lautner's theory, criticized inconclusively by G.R. Driver and J.C. Miles, *The Babylonian Laws* (Oxford: Oxford University Press, 1952-55), 1:74-76.

Bearing this contrast in mind, one may return to the question that provoked this excursus into the courts of Mesopotamia. Does the semantic field to which *dikē* as substantive right and *timē* belong have a counterpart in Near Eastern thought? To put the matter more precisely, did each member of a Mesopotamian community have a status consequent upon his inherent quality (*timē*), or was his condition assigned to him by a chain of authority descending from the king?

For the context of jurisdiction the question can be restated thus: when a Mesopotamian court gave judgment for a litigant, did it recognize his inherent right to the thing in dispute, or did it create his right by an exercise of the authority deputed to it by the king? The centralized character of judicial authority points to the second alternative. This conclusion may derive some support from the Old Babylonian practice of giving the successful litigant a record of the judgment as his title to the thing hitherto in dispute. This practice suggests that the judgment did not merely recognize a right springing from other instruments; for if so, the judgment would have had no greater force than the instruments on which the right was based, and it would have had merely provisional value until the adversary discovered instruments of still greater authority. It is more likely that the judgment created the successful litigant's right by an exercise of the royal will.

Confirmation for this reconstruction of Mesopotamian thought can perhaps be found in the Babylonian Epic of Creation (*Enuma Elish*).[41] The story tells of a primordial conflict among divine beings. The conflict comes to an end when Marduk, the champion of the gods, overcomes the monster, Tiamat. Thereupon Marduk assigns all the many gods to their places. The consequence of this assignment is the present and abiding order of the universe. Does his place belong to each god because of his inherent quality or because Marduk has assigned it to him? The tale invites the latter reading.

Toward the Rule of Law

Information on the administration of justice in the Near East of the Bronze Age is scanty. Much remains uncertain, even within periods for

---

41. J.B. Pritchard, *Ancient Near Eastern Texts Relating to the Old Testament,* 3d ed. (Princeton: Princeton University Press, 1969), 60–72. Tablet V, beginning with the line "He constructed stations for the great gods," is relevant here. Hesiod (*Theog.* 885) presents the same theme with brevity.

which the extant evidence has been deciphered and studied. But that material is consistent in presenting Mesopotamian justice as despotic. All judicial authority was derived from the king, and the conclusion is probable, though not fully certain, that the rights of each subject were conferred on him from above. Two stories told by Herodotos illustrate the persistence of a despotic conception of justice in the Near East. The one story tells of Deiokes the Mede. He won the confidence of his fellow countrymen by the wisdom he showed as a mediator when disputants chose him to judge their differences. So they made him their king. Then he shut himself off in a palace with strong walls and a bodyguard, he brought the Medes together into a fortified city, and he did not allow his subjects to see him but required them to deal with him through messengers.[42] The despot, being the source of authority and decisions, makes himself inaccessible to his subjects.

The other story, that of the wife of Intaphrenes, also presents a king who is inaccessible behind walls. After Intaphrenes and the men of his house had been arrested, his wife went "to the door of the king" and wept. Through a messenger Dareios inquired who she was and what moved her to weep.[43] The Persians had adopted practices of government from earlier rulers of the Near East. In Mesopotamian texts, the gate is often mentioned as the place where a court sits.[44] In Babylon "the gate of Marduk" is a place of administration and jurisdiction.[45] The ruler is generally inaccessible, but on occasion he or his messenger may receive petitions and grant favors at his door or gate. The same image persisted in the East for a long time. While French was the international language, European diplomats in Constantinople were accredited to the Sublime Porte. Again, the Indo-European root of the word *door* is preserved in the first syllable of the *durbar* of an Indian prince.

The semantic field to which *dikē* and surely *timē* belong offers a

---

42. Hdt. 1.96–100.
43. Hdt. 3.119. A motif from this story appears also in Soph. *Ant.* 905–12. The Herodotean reference to the door shows which direction the borrowing took. Commentators on Sophokles have rightly given much attention to the outcome of the story. For the present purpose it illustrates the theme of a king whom his subjects can only approach through intermediaries.
44. W. von Soden, *Einführung in die Altorientalistik* (Darmstadt: Wissenschaftliche Buchgesellschaft, 1985), 134.
45. Walther, *Altbabylonisches Gerichtswesen,* 261. Kafka borrowed the Near Eastern significance of the door in his story of the man who came from the countryside to seek admission to the law and was confronted by a door-keeper (*Der Prozess,* chap. 9).

conception of an orderly society contrasting with that current in the Near East. That field includes the normative concept of the portion that belongs to each person in consequence of his inherent quality. When the Achaians had carried out a successful raid shortly before the opening of the *Iliad,* they shared out the booty in accordance with each man's worth. Achilles became aggrieved because Agamemnon disregarded his *timē* in taking away his prize. When Menelaos and Antilochos quarreled over the second prize in the chariot race, Antilochos yielded in deference to the superior standing of the other claimant. Antilochos said in apology that he had acted in the folly of youth; "but thou art older and better."[46] Age contributed to the greater *timē* of Menelaos. Within each community, as portrayed in the *Iliad* and the *Odyssey,* every member had his own *timē,* a status differing from that of all other members. Only the vagrant, who came from outside and had no place in the community, had no *timē* (cf. at n. 31 above).

In historic Greece, and in particular in Athens where conditions can be best discerned, there arose the concept of the member of the community who has the plenitude of privileges. This egalitarian concept was fostered when judicial litigation superseded unrestricted self-help. When parties are compelled to go to law, the court creates an artificial equality between them, at least for the duration of the trial. The outcome of self-help results from the differing degrees of power exercised by the parties in the community. The court sets that factor aside and directs its whole attention to the defined issue that is put before it. Consequently, in each city of Greece, the adult male citizens were the members of the community who enjoyed all the privileges of membership. They were a minority among the persons belonging to the community. Others, notably women, children, and resident aliens, had rights of lesser extent. But the adult male citizens were equal among themselves. For they had their status, not because it had been conferred on them by a higher power, but because of their inherent quality as members of the community in the highest degree. This status was their *timē*. Once recourse to litigation for settlement of disputes had become compulsory, *timē* no longer varied from one person to another, as in Homeric thought; it was shared equally among adult male citizens.[47] If such a person was deprived of legal protection and outlawed, he became *atimos;* that is, he lost *timē*.

---

46. *Il.* 23.588. On *timē* as proper apportionment in the *Iliad* see G. Nagy, *The Best of the Achaeans* (Baltimore: Johns Hopkins University Press, 1979), 131–34.

47. In the *Odyssey,* Alkinoos and the Phaiakians accorded *timē* to Arete without incongruity (7.66-72). But in the heroic tragedies of Sophokles and Euripides, only manly

As already noted, the classical Greeks did not produce a corpus of juristic literature. Even so, the concepts and aims—or, to speak more loosely, the principles—discernible in their institutions are a body of thought that guided the development of law. Indeed they engaged in discussions of juristic type, and some of these are reflected in writings of Aristotle. Part of his observations on justice in the *Ethics* (5.1129a3-37a30) calls for note here. He distinguishes two senses, general and special, of "justice" (*dikaiosynē*). In the general sense it means observance of everything that is lawful. He proceeds to consider the special sense more fully. That justice has a special sense is evident from this, that although some unjust acts, such as deeds of cowardice, irascibility, and avarice, offend against other precepts—for example of valor, equanimity, and liberality—other unjust acts contravene precepts of justice alone. Injustice in the special sense consists in taking excessive amounts of honor or wealth.

Aristotle further distinguishes justice in the special sense into two kinds, distributive and rectificatory (1130b30-31a9). The latter operates in dealings between people. These are of two kinds, voluntary and involuntary. Voluntary dealings are transactions such as purchase and sale, loan and hire of various kinds. Involuntary dealings are delicts, such as theft, false testimony, injury to the person, and homicide. Distributive justice has to do with honor, wealth, and the other things that are to be shared among the members of the political community. Aristotle adds that everyone agrees that these are to be distributed according to the worth (*axia*) of the recipients, but people of different political convictions assert different criteria of worth. The *dēmokratikoi* recognize only free status (*eleutheria*) as the criterion; others recognize wealth, good birth, or personal merit (1131a25-29).

Thus in Aristotle's view good things are to be distributed among the members of the community not at the discretion of a ruling power but in the light of a criterion to be discerned among those members, even though the criterion may vary from one community to another. Likewise rectificatory justice does not respect persons, in the modern phrase; as Aristotle says:

> It makes no difference whether an upright man cheated a man of inferior character or a man of inferior character cheated an upright

---

women, such as Medeia, are concerned for their *timē;* cf. E.B. Bongie, "Heroic Elements in the Medea of Euripides," *TAPhA* 107 (1977): 27-56, especially 29. *Timē* had come to be reserved for men.

man, or whether adultery was committed by an upright man or by a man of inferior character; the law regards only the degree of the injury and it treats people as equals, asking whether one has inflicted and the other has suffered injustice, or whether one has inflicted and the other has suffered loss. (1132a2-6)

Aristotle recognized that justice has to do with apportioning things and with rectifying wrongful apportionments. Many centuries later apportionment was recognized as central to justice in the opening sentence of the *Institutes* of Justinian: "Justice is an abiding and permanent intention of according to each his due" (1.1 = *Digest* 1.1.10 "iustitia est constans et perpetua voluntas ius suum cuique tribuens"). To discover what each one's due is, the jurists of Justinian compiled the *Code,* the *Digest,* and the *Novellae,* and later jurists compiled commentaries, which the emperor had forbidden. The enterprise of developing the law can continue indefinitely. Rome carried this enterprise much further than any Greek city is known to have done. The heritage of Roman legal thought was bequeathed to modern systems both of the Civil and of the Common Law.[48] Roman law cannot be shown to have derived anything from Greek law. But like the Romans, the Greeks recognized the rule of law. It was embedded in the normative words of their Indo-European vocabulary.

In an earlier essay the present author maintained that the Athenians had a conception of the rule of law and created institutions to achieve it.[49] Going further, the present essay has looked for a Greek conception of the rule of law and has claimed to discover the impulse toward it in some ideas common to the Indo-European languages. For the sake of precision some words of caution need to be uttered. First, the concept of law, justice, or right may vary among societies that recognize that concept. As observed at the end of chapter 4, the reasons for preferring

---

48. The influence of Roman law on English law in its early stages is real, though limited; see H.J. Wolff, *Roman Law: An Historical Introduction* (Norman: University of Oklahoma Press), 197-98.

49. Sealey, *Athenian Republic,* 146. Reviewers (e.g., D. Whitehead, *Times Literary Supplement,* January 15-21, 1988, p. 68; M.H. Hansen, *Gnomon* 61 [1989]: 744-46; C. Mossé, *EMC,* n.s., 9 [1990]: 74-77; J. Ober, *Modern Greek Studies Yearbook* 4 [1988]: 309-12, cf. idem, *Mass and Elite in Democratic Athens* [Princeton: Princeton University Press, 1989], 303-4) have been shocked. My thesis may have been true or false; one reviewer (A. Kränzlein, *ZSR* 107 [1990]: 462-70) rightly observes that the Athenians did not create another institution, the learned jurist, which could have gone further to achieve the rule of law. But my thesis was not shocking.

litigation to self-help were not the same in classical Greece as in modern societies. Each society, if it recognizes the rule of law, has its own way of conceiving a society ordered by law.

Again, the rule of law contrasts with arbitrary government. Arbitrary regimes of centralized type have ruled much of the world in most of its recorded history. In them the central power is the sole focus of loyalty and therefore the sole source of authority. It may confer rights on its subjects, but their rights are derivative and precarious; they cannot withstand the central power. Such regimes are often classified under the heading, "oriental despotism."[50] But they have not been confined to the East and in the East they have not been universal; notably Japan has traditionally had focuses of loyalty, and therefore sources of authority, independent of the central government. Consequently this essay does not assert that the rule of law can only be achieved in nations inheriting Indo-European concepts. It maintains merely that the rule of law has sometimes sprung from those concepts.

---

50. K. Wittfogel, *Oriental Despotism* (New Haven: Yale University Press, 1957) is still a serviceable introduction. Critics have found fault with Wittfogel's attempt to explain why despotic regimes arose; they have not doubted the despotic character of the regimes studied.

Bibliography

Amira, K. von, and Eckhardt, K.A. *Germanisches Recht*. 2 vols., 4th ed. Berlin: de Gruyter, 1960, 1967.
Bähr, P. *Grundzüge des bürgerlichen Rechts*. 7th ed. Munich: Vahlen, 1989.
Calhoun, G.M. *The Growth of Criminal Law in Ancient Greece*. Berkeley: University of California Press, 1927.
Cartledge, P.; Millett, P.; and Todd, S., eds. *Nomos: Essays in Athenian Law, Politics and Society*. Cambridge: Cambridge University Press, 1990.
Chambers, M. *Aristoteles: Staat der Athener*. Berlin: Akademie Verlag, 1990.
Cruveilhier, P. "Le lévirat chez les Hébreux et chez les Assyriens." *Revue Biblique* 34 (1925): 524–46.
Driver, G.R., and Miles, J.C. *The Assyrian Laws*. Oxford: Oxford University Press, 1935; reprinted with additions by Driver, at Aalen, 1975.
Driver, G.R., and Miles, J.C. *The Babylonian Laws*. 2 vols. Oxford: Oxford University Press, 1952, 1955.
Dworkin, R. *Law's Empire*. Cambridge, MA: Belknap, 1986.
Falkenstein, A. *Die neusumerischen Gerichtsurkunden 1: Einleitung und systematische Darstellung*. Munich: Bayerische Akademie der Wissenschaften, 1956.
Finkelstein, J.J. "Ammiṣaduqa's Edict and the Babylonian 'Law Codes'." *Journal of Cuneiform Studies* 15 (1961): 91–104.
Finkelstein, J.J. "Some New *Misharum* Material and Its Implications." *Assyriological Studies* 16 (1965): 233–46.
Finkelstein, J.J. "Sex Offences in Sumerian Laws." *Journal of the American Oriental Society* 86 (1966): 355–72.
Friedrich, J. *Die hethitischen Gesetze*. Leiden: Brill, 1959.
Frier, B.W. *The Rise of the Roman Jurists: Studies in Cicero's "pro Caecina."* Princeton: Princeton University Press, 1985.
Gagarin, M. *Drakon and Early Athenian Homicide Law*. New Haven: Yale University Press, 1981.
Gagarin, M. *Early Greek Law*. Berkeley: University of California Press, 1986.
Harrison, A.R.W. *The Law of Athens*. 2 vols. Vol. 1, *The Family and Property*. Vol. 2, *Procedure*. Oxford: Oxford University Press, 1968–71.

Henrich, D. *Einführung in das englische Privatrecht.* 2d ed. Darmstadt: Wissenschaftliche Buchgesellschaft, 1993.
Kränzlein, A. *Eigentum und Besitz im griechischen Recht des fünften und vierten Jahrhunderts v. Chr.* Berlin: Duncker, 1963.
Lautner, J.G. *Die richterliche Entscheidung und die Streitbeendigung im altbabylonischen Prozessrechte.* Leipzig: Weicher, 1922.
Leage, R.W. *Roman Private Law.* 3d ed. rev. A.M. Prichard. London: Macmillan, 1961.
Lipsius, J.H. *Das attische Recht und Rechtsverfahren.* 3 vols. Leipzig: Reisland, 1905-15.
Maine, H.S. *Ancient Law.* 1861. Reprint, London: Dent, 1965.
Meiggs, R., and Lewis, D. *A Selection of Greek Historical Inscriptions to the End of the Fifth Century* B.C. Oxford: Oxford University Press, 1969.
Nicholas, B. *An Introduction to Roman Law.* Oxford: Oxford University Press, 1962.
Ostwald, M. *From Popular Sovereignty to the Sovereignty of Law.* Berkeley: University of California Press, 1986.
Pritchard, J.B. *Ancient Near Eastern Texts Relating to the Old Testament.* 3d ed. Princeton: Princeton University Press, 1969.
Rawls, J. *A Theory of Justice.* Cambridge, MA: Belknap, 1971.
Rhodes, P.J. *A Commentary on the Aristotelian "Athenaion Politeia."* Oxford: Oxford University Press, 1981.
Ruschenbusch, E. "*Phonos.* Zum Recht Drakons und seiner Bedeutung für das Werden des athenischen Staates." *Historia* 9 (1960): 129-54.
Ruschenbusch, E. "*Ephesis.* Ein Beitrag zur griechischen Rechtsterminologie." *ZSR* 78 (1961): 386-90.
Ruschenbusch, E. "*Hybreōs graphē.*" *ZSR* 82 (1965): 302-9.
Ruschenbusch, E. "*Hēliaia.* Die Tradition über das solonische Volksgericht." *Historia* 14 (1965): 381-84.
Ruschenbusch, E. "*Solonos Nomoi.*" *Die Fragmente des solonischen Gesetzeswerkes mit einer Text- und Überlieferungsgeschichte.* Wiesbaden: Steiner, 1968.
Ruschenbusch, E. *Untersuchungen zur Geschichte des athenischen Strafrechts.* Cologne: Böhlau, 1968.
Ruschenbusch, E. "*Dikē kata tinos* und *pros tina.*" *ZSR* 86 (1969): 386-94.
Sealey, R. "How Citizenship and the City Began in Athens." *AJAH* 8 (1983): 97-129.
Sealey, R. *The Athenian Republic: Democracy or the Rule of Law?* University Park: Pennsylvania State University Press, 1987.
Sealey, R. *Women and Law in Classical Greece.* Chapel Hill: University of North Carolina Press, 1990.
Soden, W. von. *Einführung in die Altorientalistik.* Darmstadt: Wissenschaftliche Buchgesellschaft, 1985.
Stroud, R.S. *Drakon's Law on Homicide.* Berkeley: University of California Press, 1968.
Thür, G. "Zum *dikazein* bei Homer." *ZSR* 87 (1970): 426-44.

Thür, G. "Die Todesstrafe im Blutprozess Athens." *Journal of Juristic Papyrology* 20 (1990): 143–56.
Tod, M.N. *A Selection of Greek Historical Inscriptions.* Vol. 2. Oxford: Oxford University Press, 1948.
Walther, A. *Das altbabylonische Gerichtswesen.* Leipzig: Hinrichs, 1917.
Watson, A. *The Law of Persons in the Later Roman Republic.* Oxford: Oxford University Press, 1967.
Watson, A. *The Law of Property in the Later Roman Republic.* Oxford: Oxford University Press, 1968.
Watson, A. *The Evolution of Law.* Baltimore: Johns Hopkins University Press, 1985.
Whitehead, D. *The Ideology of the Athenian Metic.* Cambridge: Cambridge University Press, 1977.
Willetts, R.F. *The Law Code of Gortyn.* Berlin: de Gruyter, 1967.
Wolff, H.J. "The Origin of Judicial Litigation among the Greeks." *Traditio* 4 (1946): 31–87.
Wolff, H.J. *Roman Law: An Historical Introduction.* Norman: University of Oklahoma Press, 1951.

Index

Achilles, 92, 96-100, 142, 144, 152; shield of, 103-4, 111, 115
actio aquae pluviae arcendae, 59-60
actio rei uxoriae, 77
adoption, 18, 21, 70-72, 81, 87, 121
adultery, 110, 126, 128
Aeskil Magnusson, 29
Agamemnon, 96, 98-100, 142, 144, 152
agnate, 53, 74, 83, 87
aidesis, 118
Aischylos, 64
Aitolia, 52
Akkad, 31, 146
alien, 61, 88, 152. *See also* metics
Ammiṣaduqa, 31
anakrisis, 105, 109, 119-20, 127, 134, 136
anchisteis, 75, 87
Andokides, 45-48
Antilochos, 92-95, 98-99, 101, 105, 147, 152
antōmosia, 136
Antoninus Pius, 3
Anu, 31
apagōgē, 127
apographē, 127
Apollo, 28, 92, 99
apophasis, 127
arbitration, 108, 137-38
archon, 68, 105, 113-15
Areopagos, 123, 127
Aristophanes, 27, 120
Aristotle, 15, 25-26, 28-29, 43, 53, 57, 59, 116, 123, 130, 153-54
Arthmios, 12
Aššur, 33

atimia, 12-13, 20-21, 27, 118, 123, 127-28, 130, 152
Austin, John, 6-7, 21

Babylon, 145, 147-51
basileis, 113-15
battle, trial by, 106-7
Bentham, Jeremy, 6
bequest, 3, 14-15, 18, 21, 44, 70-71, 87, 121, 124
betrothal, 34, 62

Charondas, 25-28
Cicero, 5-6
citizenship, 44, 61, 64, 66-68, 73, 88, 133-34
code, 10, 30-50, 55, 121, 133; German, 10-11; Near Eastern, 30-37; of 403, 44-50; of Napoleon, 10, 22n37
coemptio, 77, 87
contract, 7, 61-62
conveyance, 2, 62, 66, 73, 77
Corinth, 25
Crete, 25, 27, 37, 73
crime, 42, 125-32
Cyprus, 10, 114

Dareios, 151
debt, 13, 15, 17, 124-25
Deiokes, 151
delict, 43, 61, 125, 132
Delphi, 28
Demonax, 26
Demosthenes, 12-13, 15-16, 60, 117-18, 120, 124

161

Index 162

Dikaiogenes, 69
dikastai, 51, 105, 116, 119–20, 137–38
dikastērion, 109, 120–21, 127, 135, 137–38
dikē, 92–93, 100–105, 119, 122, 127–29, 138–41, 151; *aphaireseōs eis eleutherian,* 124, 126; *apostasiou,* 65; *aprostasiou,* 65; *biaiōn,* 126; *exoulēs,* 110, 124, 126; *kata tinos,* 125; *pros tina,* 125
Diodoros, 26
Diokles, 26–28
Diomedes, 92
divorce, 38, 68n.30, 77–78, 80
dowry, 17, 77–80
Drakon, 28, 43–45, 47, 49, 116–17
droit, 4

edict, 136
eisangelia, 127, 129–30
ekdosis, 67–68, 77–78
Eleusis, 27
endeixis, 127
engyēsis, 67–69, 77, 79, 87
Enlil, 31
ephēboi, 73
ephēgēsis, 127
ephetai, 116–20
epidikasia, 68
epiklēros, 15–21, 68, 83, 86–87, 128
Epikouros, 15
Epikteta, 82–83
equality, 152
Eresos, 52
Eshnunna, 30
Eumaios, 140, 144
Eumelos, 92
Eurymachos, 144
executor, 14

field, semantic, 4, 133, 140–41, 145, 151–52
Finkelstein, J.J., 30–34
Finley, Sir Moses, 67–69
formula, 136, 139
France, 10
fraud, 41

Gaius, 3, 53, 60
gens, 74
Gesetz, 4
Gortyn, 29, 37–43, 63, 67, 69–72, 76, 79–82, 84, 87–88

graphē, 127–31; *adikōs heirchthēnai hōs moichon,* 110, 128; *asebeias,* 131; *dōrōn,* 130; *hybreōs,* 53, 129; *klopēs dēmosiōn chrēmatōn,* 131; *klopēs hierōn chrēmatōn,* 131; *nomon mē epitēdeion theinai,* 50, 130; *paranomōn,* 49–50, 130; *parapresbeias,* 130; *pseudoklēteias,* 122; *xenias,* 131
gynē, 19

Hammurapi, 31–32
heiress, 17, 38, 69, 79. See also *epiklēros; patrōiōkos*
Hektor, 107
hēliaia, 119–22
Hera, 97–100
Herodotos, 28, 43, 84, 100
Herondas, 26
Hesiod, 102, 107, 114–15, 119
Hieron, 26
Hobbes, Thomas, 6
Homer, 27, 65, 114
homicide, 12–13, 43, 75, 110, 116–19, 123
horkia, 97n.9, 99
house-purchase, 61–62
hybris, 53, 129
Hypereides, 129

Iceland, 29
Iliad, 92–107, 114–15, 119, 138–39, 141, 143, 152
Indo-European, 24, 141, 154–55
inheritance, 7, 13–20, 53, 61, 67–76, 79–80
Intaphrenes, 151
Ithaka, 115, 139, 143
iudex, 136
ius, 4

Japan, 10, 155
joinder of the issue, 104, 110, 119, 136
Juda, 86
judges: at Athens, 51; at Gortyn, 41, 51
jurisconsults, 13, 53–54, 57, 137
jurists, 8, 36; Roman, 5, 8, 54, 60, 154
justice, 1, 3–4, 23, 133–34, 153–55
Justinian, 11, 14, 154

Kalchas, 99
Katane, 25
Kephalos, 26, 28
kings: Hittite, 36; mediaeval, 42, 111

kinship, 61, 67, 71, 74-76
klēros, 15
Konon, 15
kosmopolis, 56-57
Kyrene, 26, 73
kyrios, 18-19, 69, 77-79, 81-82, 88, 129

Lagash, 145-46
law, 1-4, 22-24, 133-34, 138, 154-55; Assyrian, 33-35; Athenian, 12-19, 43-51; book of, 10-11, 29, 36; Civil, 10, 19-20, 54, 60, 154; Common, 10, 12, 14, 19-20, 54, 154; customary, 8, 11; Gortynian, 37-43, 51, 70-72, 76, 84, 126; German, 29; Germanic, 95-96, 106-7; Hebrew, 70, 85-87; Hittite, 35-37; Mesopotamian, 30-33, 105-6, 145-50; natural, 5-6; Near Eastern, 30-37; private, 23, 44; public, 44; Roman, 3, 11, 13-14, 16, 20-21, 53-55, 60, 72, 74, 76-79, 84, 136-38; rule of, 22-24, 150-55
lawgivers, 25-30, 44-45, 48-49
lawsuit, 32, 39-40, 125-31
legis actio sacramento, 96, 106
lex, 4, 55; *Cornelia,* 136
limitation, 63
Lipit-Ishtar, 30-32
litigation, compulsory, 107-11
Lokroi, 25, 55-57, 63
loi, 4
Lumbaer, 29
Lykourgos, 28
Lysias, 45

majority, attainment of, 2, 88
mancipatio per aes et libram, 62, 66, 72, 77
manus, 72, 76-79, 82-83, 87
manus iniectio, 40, 124
Marduk, 150-51
marriage, 2-3, 7, 61, 67-70, 76-81, 84; levirate, 70, 85-87
mashkim, 146
Megara, 27
Menelaos, 92-95, 98-99, 101, 105-6, 143, 147, 152
metics, 64-66, 88
Miletos, 26
Minos, 25
misharum-act, 31-33

nation, 8-9
Naupaktos, 52
Nikomachos, 44-45
Nippur, 30
nomoi, 43-45, 49-50, 116
Norway, 29
nothoi, 67-68

oath, 92-93, 95-101, 104-6, 146-48; of Athenian judges, 51, 122
Odysseus, 97, 99, 107, 115-16, 139-40, 144
Odyssey, 65, 97-99, 115, 138-40
offenses, 41-43, 125-32; sexual, 126
oikos, 14-17, 21, 70, 88
orphan, 128; female, 17-19, 38, 61, 69, 79, 83-88

Palmer, L.R., 140-41, 145
paragraphē, 134-37
Paris, 106
Paros, 25
Pasion, 15
pater familias, 73-74, 77-79, 82-83, 87-88
patria potestas, 72, 74, 76-77, 82-83
patrōiōkos, 79, 84, 87-88
Patroklos, 92, 94, 142
Pausanias, 114
peirar, 103
Peisistratos, 116
Penelope, 139-40
penalties, 35-36, 42-43, 125-27
Phaiakia, 114
phasis, 127
Phile, 69
Philolaos, 25, 27-28
pignoris capio, 40, 124
Plato, 15
Plutarch, 28
poinē, 103, 118
polemarch, 68
polis, 144
Polybios, 55
Polydoros, 26, 28
Poseidon, 93, 99
possession, 55-57, 62
praetor, 14, 53, 136-37, 139
prescription, 62-63, 77
primogeniture, 5
proof, mode of, 100-7
property, 60, 63, 66
prosecutor, voluntary, 127-31

prostatēs, 65
Pyrrhos, 69

ransom, 125-26
Recht, 4, 133
Rechtsbuch, 11, 36
Repchow, Eike von, 10
Rhadamanthys, 25
right, 1, 3-4, 23, 133-34, 154
Ruth, 85

Sachsenspiegel, 10-11, 36
Savigny, Friedrich Carl von, 6-11, 20-21
security, 124
seisachtheia, 64, 122, 124
seizure, 38-40, 124-25
self-help, 75, 107-11, 124-25, 127, 152, 155
seller's liability, 2-3
serf, 39
Shamash, 31
Shulgi, 32
slavery, 38-40, 61, 63-66
Solon, 15, 27-29, 43, 45, 47, 49-50, 64-66, 116, 120-25, 127-28
sovereign, 6
Sparta, 28, 73, 84
status, 61, 63-67
statute, 9
stipulatio, 62
Styx, 97
succession: intestate, 14, 68-71, 74-76; universal, 13-16, 20-21, 61, 70
sui iuris, 18, 72-73, 77, 79, 83
Sumer, 31 145-47
Sweden, 29
Syracuse, 26-27

talion, 108
Teisamenos, 45-49, 116
Telemachos, 97, 139
Thamar, 86
Thebes, 25, 27
Thera, 82-83
thesmoi, 29, 43, 45, 116, 122, 130
thesmothetai, 29
Thibaut, A.F.J., 8
Thourioi, 26
Thucydides, 46
timē, 142-45, 150-52
Timoleon, 26
treaties, Greek, 96
tutela, tutor, 18, 83
Twelve Tables, 55, 59-60, 74, 95
tyranny, 123, 130

Ur, 30, 145
Ur-Nammu, 30, 32, 146
United States, Constitution of, 9

voluntary, 93-95, 101, 104, 153

Watson, A., 102
wergild, 103, 118
Westgötaland, 29
will, 2, 7, 13-16, 19-20, 70, 81-82; mancipatory, 72-73, 87; praetorian, 72, 87
Wolff, H. J., 109, 116, 126-27
women, 18-19, 67-69, 76-83, 88, 152

Xenophon, 28

Zaleukos, 25-26, 28-29, 55
Zeus, 97, 99, 102

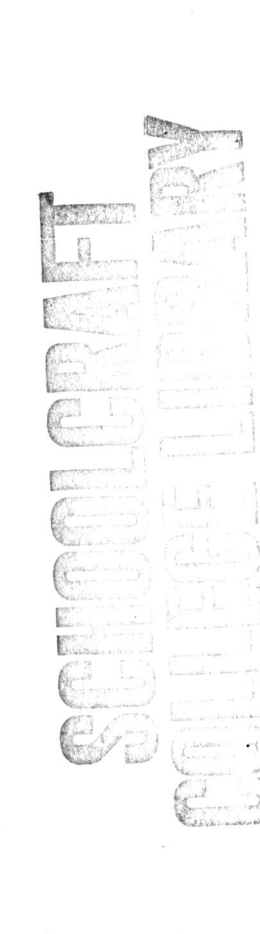